FREEDOM FROM ANGER

FREEDOM

FROM

ANGER

UNDERSTANDING IT,

OVERCOMING IT,

AND FINDING JOY

Venerable Alubomulle Sumanasara

Wisdom

Wisdom Publications
199 Elm Street
Somerville, MA 02144 USA
wisdompubs.org

Library of Congress Cataloging-in-Publication Data
Sumanasara, Alubomulle, author.
   Freedom from anger : understanding it, overcoming it, and finding joy / Ven. Alubomulle Sumanasara.
      pages cm
   ISBN 1-61429-224-8 (pbk. : alk. paper)
   1. Anger—Religious aspects—Buddhism. I. Title.
   BQ4570.A52S86 2015
   294.3'444—dc23

                                      2014037291

ISBN 978-1-61429-224-1   ebook ISBN 978-1-61429-240-1

19 18 17 16 15   6 5 4 3 2

Author photo on page 143 is © Harumi Aida.
Cover design by Phil Pascuzzo. Interior design by Gopa&Ted2, Inc.
Set in Garamond Premier Pro 10.8/13.6.

Wisdom Publications' books are printed on acid-free paper and meet the guidelines for permanence and durability of the Production Guidelines for Book Longevity of the Council on Library Resources.

This book was produced with environmental mindfulness. We have elected to print this title on 30% PCW recycled paper. As a result, we have saved the following resources: 4 trees, 1 million BTUs of energy, 353 lbs. of greenhouse gases, 1,912 gallons of water, and 128 lbs. of solid waste. For more information, please visit our website, wisdompubs.org.

Printed in the United States of America.

MIX
Paper from
responsible sources
FSC® C011935
www.fsc.org

Please visit fscus.org.

TABLE OF CONTENTS

II. Anger Destroys Happiness

III. Those Who Don't Get Angry

IV. The Solution to Anger

I

UNDERSTANDING ANGER

DON'T FLATTER ANGER

"It's normal to get angry."

"What's wrong with getting angry?"

"If you don't get angry, it means you aren't passionate about what you do."

THE WORLD SEEMS to be full of angry people. I'm sure you know at least a few of them; people who use strong language and act abusively, creating uncomfortable situations for others. Some people even consider the ability to get angry to be a sign of one's importance and power.

This is not good. Anger is not a trivial emotion of the mind that we can take lightly. "I became angry" is the equivalent of admitting, "I reacted foolishly, and I was a failure." Anger should be considered a serious matter.

Nowadays, many people talk about their anger freely and with little concern. It seems that they have no proper understanding of the malignant and devastating nature of anger. If you let anger inhabit your mind, you have opened yourself to a life full of suffering, failures, and unhappiness. Anything can irritate an irritable person, like a man who gets upset at grass for being green.

Sharing your life with anger is contrary to the universal law of living: humans—and every living being—seek happiness, not suffering and failure. So let us spend some time together learning about anger, the enemy of joy.

THE URGE TO GET ANGRY IS INNATE

People often tell me, "I didn't want to get angry, but somehow I just did…" The solution to this problem is very straightforward, simple, and complete: Don't get angry. Let go of anger. Just blow it out.

It's actually quite obvious, isn't it? Don't get angry, and you won't be an angry person. There's no other solution.

Some of you may be thinking, "That's true! All I need to do is not get angry. I'll just stop." If you truly understand and believe this, then you have learned the lesson and can stop reading this book now, and go and live a happy life. Well done!

But most people who hear this advice simply reply, "I know that already, but I can't stop. That's why I'm asking for help." Such people, you see, naturally give in to anger, whenever and wherever, as much as they like. But they also know somewhere inside themselves that they should not be reacting in that way, they know that to become angry is wrong, and so they look for a way to resolve this internal conflict.

Everyone occasionally feels a strong urge to get angry. But before surrendering to anger, just observe the internal conflict of your mind. If you pay attention, you'll find that there is a warning signal against being angry, but people fail to heed it. Out of the two urges—get angry or resist anger—people easily select the first choice. Then, in order to feel better, they fool themselves and say that they didn't *want* to become angry.

You can see the truth of this, can't you? You become angry because you have given anger a free pass to overcome your other emotions whenever possible. Saying you didn't really want to be angry is dishonest. People who truly don't want to get angry do not. They take great care not to. They can maintain their composure. Only a very few things can upset them. Even if they do become upset about something, they immediately feel shame and correct their behavior.

Buddhism has no interest in finding tricks for disguising or diverting anger. Life is short and should be spent on working to make oneself a better person; there is no time to fool around with one's own life. Do you seek happiness? If you do, then you should begin by admitting, "Sometimes I do want to get angry. I am not perfect."

The next step is then to learn about anger: what it is and why it happens. Understanding the problem is the first step toward solving it.

LIFE IS GOVERNED BY ANGER AND LOVE

When the Buddha taught about anger, he began by defining it clearly.

Anger, like love, is an emotion that can manifest suddenly in the mind. When we see our family or loved ones, the feeling of attachment and love quickly arises. Similarly, eating when you are hungry, or even looking at delicious food, can also give rise to immediate pleasure. In the same way, anger can appear instantly, seemingly without warning.

Our lives are defined by these two emotions: love (which can give rise to attachment) and anger. These are the motive forces of our lives; they are the two sides of the same coin. Now it should be quite easy to understand the nature of anger. Your life, like a coin, cannot stand vertically; it has to show either heads or tails.

If you want a simple test for whether you are angry at any given moment, ask yourself, "Do I feel good? Am I happy right now?" If the answer is "Not especially" or even "I'm bored," then you have anger lurking somewhere within you. Boredom and displeasure are symptoms of anger. When you feel pleasure, happiness, or positive excitement, then you cannot be angry. A sense of well-being indicates the absence of anger.

Please think about anger in this way—not just as a definition of the word, but as an understanding of the feeling within you—for this will allow you to recognize it better when it arises.

DIFFERENT FORMS OF ANGER

EMOTIONS CAN BECOME AMPLIFIED, and when they do they take on a new character. For this reason, we need different words to distinguish among the different degrees of the same basic emotion.

Think of it in the same way as electricity. The electrical current that flows through the wiring in our homes is not particularly strong. We even have some almost-imperceptible electricity flowing through our bodies—about enough to power a small light bulb. On the other hand, when millions of volts of energy build up as static electricity in the air and discharge, the result is a lightning strike. Although the electricity in a bolt of lightning and a nine-volt battery may appear to be very different, they are fundamentally the same phenomenon. The difference is only one of degree. Your body can absorb the weak current from a small battery without being harmed, but touching the power line that leads into your home could cause a fatal shock or start a fire. As power grows, its nature changes.

Let us now look at how this relates to anger. When you think, "I'm really bored right now," the anger you feel is not so severe. But if that same feeling were to become stronger and stronger, it can become dangerous, just like the difference between a mild spark and a thunderbolt. So just as we distinguish between a battery's weak current and lightning, we need different words for the various forms and degrees of anger. The following are Pali terms for different types of anger:

Vera (hatred; rage). Anger that becomes very strong, so strong that it makes your teeth grind, fists clench, and muscles shake.

Upanāhī (resentment; a grudge). A lasting form of anger that can persist for days, months, even an entire lifetime.

Makkhī (disdain). The feeling of those who constantly belittle others and take great pride in themselves. Vanity, and the inability to recognize other people's talent, ability, beauty, or strength without envy or begrudging.

Palāsī (spite; malice). Striving against others; the failure to work or live in harmony with other people; the desire to compete in an all-or-nothing manner, always wanting to defeat others and come out on top. This attitude of constantly challenging other people results in strife, and it too is another form of anger.

Issukī (envy; jealousy). The inability to accept when good things happen to others. When turned inward, this leads one only into darkness, joylessness, and unhappiness.

Macchari (meanness; stinginess; miserliness). This may appear to be an exaggeration of desire, but in fact it's something else entirely. Macchari is displeasure in others using and enjoying what you feel belongs to you. It means not wanting to share. This is also a state of darkness.

Dubacca (arrogance). Resistance or refusal. None of us is perfect, nor will we ever be, and so in order to grow, we must learn and take guidance from others, right up until the end of our lives. People nevertheless make excuses and struggle against accepting this truth—arrogance is another way in which anger can manifest.

Kukkucca (remorse). Regret, which some people mistakenly see as an admirable trait. But regret is different from reflecting on and learning from the past. Regret eats up one's happiness. Worrying over past mistakes occupies the mind. This dark emotion of the mind is also another form of anger.

Byāpāda (malevolence). Senseless fury, anger without reason. It can also be used to describe anger that is completely disproportionate to its cause, the anger that causes people to lash out or even to kill.

ANGER AND LOVE COME
FROM WITHIN

WHEN FEELINGS OF DARKNESS, joylessness, or unhappiness strengthen, they become unmanageable and force their way into one's behavior—they transform into hatred. At even stronger levels, such feelings have destructive effects in many aspects of one's life. The first to be affected is the self, then others. Anger is at the root of much destruction in the world, just as love is the wellspring of creation.

Anger destroys what love has made. This is a universal give-and-take—the flow of two kinds of energy. You could say that the combination of these energies of love and anger is what powers the world.

Buddhism does not deify or make avatars of emotions. In Hinduism, they say that Brahma creates and Shiva destroys; Vishnu maintains the balance of two forces until the final destruction. Hindus believe that all human emotion is suffused with divinity, and they make clear distinctions between the spheres of these two gods. The Christian God is similarly said to embody love, while malice, envy, and hate are incarnated in the Devil. Believers therefore feel that they must worship God in order to defeat Satan. Others spend much time on fruitless debate over whether or not God, or the Devil, really exists.

Personifying human feelings in the form of gods may make them easy to understand as fables, but it is impractical for truly understanding and handling one's emotions—believing these things prevents one from perceiving the true nature of the problem. For that reason, Buddhism does not make gods of emotions. If you teach using the metaphors that anger and love are deities or anthropomorphic, people may start to believe that these are somehow separate from themselves: that one is only being tempted from without, that the fault lies with another, that the self is essentially good. They avoid looking within themselves, which can cause great problems. This attitude impedes self-development.

We should not find excuses for our inherent weaknesses. Let us admit our weaknesses and work hard to correct them.

YOU MAKE COCKROACHES UGLY

WHEN WE SEE a flower, we think, "How pretty. I like looking at this." The feeling is one of acceptance. Seeing a cockroach, however, may cause revulsion and rejection. We may experience feelings like "I don't want to see that. It's disgusting. I wish it would go away."

So who is doing all this accepting and rejecting? The answer of course is your own mind. We make these decisions as we see the world around us with our eyes, hear it with our ears, and feel it with our bodies. Acceptance of something gives rise to attachment, rejection to anger. Therefore, we can see that the true source of anger lies in the individual, not in the object. Objects are neutral. A flower has no intention of making us happy; neither does a cockroach intend to cause repulsion. Every individual's perception is fixed by his or her attitude.

Let us say that all of us are wearing colored glasses. These glasses are the difference between whether one lives in the light of contentment or in the darkness of dissatisfaction. The Buddha provides instructions to remove the glasses and correct our vision, but the responsibility of actually taking the glasses off falls entirely upon the individual. Please do not wait until a mystical being intervenes. That will never happen.

A BUG IS A TREAT TO A BIRD

Roses bloom because that is their nature. They have no sense of their own beauty and take no pride in it. They don't ask to be admired and have no care for what people may think of them.

The idea that cockroaches are disgusting likewise has its source in humans, not in the bugs themselves. Indeed, can we objectively say that they are really such horrible or disgusting creatures? Perhaps not many of you have seen this, but chickens think cockroaches are delicious. They love to eat them. A hen or rooster that sees a cockroach thinks, "Hey, that looks good! Perhaps I'll eat it." The feeling is acceptance, even desire—the opposite of the revulsion that many humans feel in response to the exact same thing.

In contrast, we may accept and love a rose bush, while the chicken rejects it and becomes angered: "What is this thing? I can't eat that! It's just in the way."

PERCEPTION

IN JAPAN, lobsters are sometimes cut open and served as food while they are still alive. Their antennae twitch, and their eyestalks swivel from side to side, even as the rest of their body has been torn open and is being eaten in front of them. Lovers of Japanese cuisine may see this and think, "Mm, that looks good!"

But try showing that to a person from India or Sri Lanka. Many would be too shocked and repelled by the sight even to consider what it might taste like. This is because they have been taught to reject the idea of eating something that is still alive as excessively cruel. In Japan, however, this type of sashimi is a real delicacy and is accepted with a connoisseur's love.

I once watched a television program in which a tribal family from deep in the mountains of Africa was invited to spend time in Japan. Their Japanese host family, thinking that their guests must never have experienced much luxury (living in the wilderness as they did), made a great effort to be gracious hosts by preparing a sashimi dinner from a large fish. But the entire African family lost their appetites at the sight of it. Even though they had never experienced more than what we would consider to be a very impoverished lifestyle, the thought of this particular food repelled them, and they begged the hosts to take it away. One of the boys, who was about eighteen, rejected it with particular intensity, turning away and saying, "I can't stand to look at it. Please take it back to the kitchen!" And so the Japanese family had no choice but to end the meal before it had begun. As you can see, one's accustomed culture plays a large part in determining how one feels about all sorts of things.

Feelings, reactions, and judgments about right and wrong can be influenced by factors such as education, the environment one grew up in, or the media. Are there not times when you hear that something is popular and you think of it as desirable, regardless of its actual quality? Black clothing, for instance, is not inherently remarkable, but at times when it's popular, people start to think, "Black is cool!" and you can see people wearing black everywhere. When people are told that some particular color or style is in, they look at it in a different way, engendering feelings of acceptance and love.

YOU HAVE THE POWER TO BE HAPPY

As you can see, our feelings are subject to powerful influences from the outside world. But, to be clear, information from the outside world by itself does not orient our attitude; we do. We are free to accept or resist or disregard external influence.

I assume that now we can understand the responsibility of the individual. Acceptance or rejection lies within ourselves. Every decision to feel love or anger is up to the person. Becoming angry is never someone else's doing; anger is always one's own fault.

If we look at this a certain way, we can see that this is good news, or at least a glimmer of light in the darkness. For you have the power to free your mind from anger and choose only to feel love and happiness. This is truly possible. Buddhism teaches that those of us who have been born human should make this our ultimate goal.

WE GET ANGRY BECAUSE
WE THINK WE ARE RIGHT

WHY DO WE GET angry when we know that it's better not to? There are many reasons that people become angry, but if we look at them all, they share a common trait: a person deciding to become angry based on his or her own arbitrary preferences or judgments.

People tend to believe that they are right, and so they become angry with anyone who disagrees with them. If you think the other person is right, you will not get angry. Remember this. We feel anger because we think, "I am right. Other people are wrong."

Though, of course, someone who tends toward anger might also get angry when he realizes that the other guy is right—because he feels he is the only one who ought to be right.

But what of instances in which a person becomes angry at himself? In fact, this is exactly the same. People can become furious at themselves when they fail to accomplish something they set out to do or when things don't go as they wish, and in both cases they are angry because they thought they were right. People get upset with themselves when things don't go well at work or at home, thinking, "But I'm perfect and experienced! How could I spoil that recipe?" or "I never make mistakes at work. How could I let this happen?"

THE "I AM RIGHT" ATTITUDE
IS CONCEALED

Does this attitude of always being right make any sense? Are we even aware of this attitude? If I were to walk up to someone and ask, "Would you say that you are perfect? That you are always correct?" the person would undoubtedly say something like, "No, of course not. I make mistakes all the time!" But then if I said, "Oh, so you're just another fool?" you can be sure he would get angry. I would have hurt that person's feelings. You can see the paradox here. People will admit to being flawed and imperfect out of humility as a matter of course, but inside themselves they are thinking all the while, "I don't believe it for a second. I'm never wrong. Everybody else is." This feeling, this attitude, does not reveal itself and appear in our consciousness. It works in the background of our mind.

Think about it—mothers get angry with their children, teachers with students, and bosses with their staff. The children, students, and employees may indeed be doing something wrong, but the mothers, teachers, and bosses seek to normalize their anger while they yell: "You did something wrong, so I'm mad at you!" In fact, it would be enough just to smile and say, "You made a mistake here. Please don't do it again." So why get angry? It's because people believe that they are correct, that their words are perfectly clear and true, as are their thoughts.

YOU WON'T GET ANGRY IF YOU KNOW
THAT YOU MIGHT BE WRONG

THE BELIEF THAT we're always right is mistaken; we need to realize that there's no way that can be. Everyone should make an effort to do this as soon as they can. Erroneous beliefs in one's fundamental correctness or infallibility are dangerous and should be rejected at once.

Humans are imperfect. Intelligent people know that they may well be wrong. They think, "I have such and such an opinion, but admittedly my understanding is not perfect."

We're also fallible in the way we communicate. The words we use are themselves limited, as are the metaphors we employ to represent reality. None of it is perfect or complete.

People may become upset when one of their children or students or employees makes a mistake, but they should realize that the true cause of their anger may have been a failure in the way they explained something. With this attitude, one can see that the fault is on both sides. It's important for people to understand that the idea that they are unerringly correct is irrational, unrealistic, and untrue. There can be no greater fool than one who believes in his own perfection. Once people accept in their hearts that they too make mistakes, they will lose their sense of irritation. Once they truly believe that they are imperfect, incomplete, and rife with error, anger will no longer arise.

Our conscious minds know that we are not perfect and that we are not always correct. Our unconscious minds, which control our behavior and personalities, maintain the opposite opinion and act accordingly. It is necessary to stop this conflict. I suggest that everybody spend some time contemplating this conflict and repeatedly advising the unconsciousness to behave.

WORDS ARE IMPERFECT

THE "PERFECTED ONE" is an epithet of the Buddha. He was not born perfect but achieved perfection and then taught the method he used to mankind; this method is Buddhism. Buddhists believe that the perfected Buddha did not have flaws in his character, that his wisdom was without fault.

You may or may not believe this yourself—that is fine. The Buddha's wisdom can still help you let go of anger and live a life of happiness.

If you read the sutras, you will see that the Buddha took great care in his use of language. He was never loose in his expressions and thought carefully about his choice of words. But words themselves are imperfect vehicles of meaning, so there were times when he was misunderstood, despite the great care he took. A man once came to the Buddha and said, "Explain to me the essence of your teachings in just a few words." The Buddha said he would and, using only a few words, made his explanation: "I teach the method of achieving absolute freedom of entire conceptualization of the mind, which is the final end of all conflicts, including quarrels, debates, fighting, taking weapons, and the final end of suffering."

Of course, there was no way for the man to be able to understand this, and he became angry, saying, "What kind of nonsense is this?" and left. Most people would have gotten angry with the man; after all, it was he who asked the impossible to begin with. But the Buddha was unperturbed. He calmly explained to the *bhikkhus* (disciples), "A man came, he asked me this question, became angry when I answered, and left," as if nothing out of the ordinary had happened.

What we can learn from this episode is that it's impossible, even for the Buddha, to speak with perfect clarity. The Buddha knew this and thought it was natural for the man to become upset and leave. He did not become angry that the man did not understand his teaching.

When his followers would ask the Buddha to explain the meaning of his words, he would do so at length, for the meaning was profound. A mother may shout at her child, "How many times do I have to tell you the same thing?" She may have to keep repeating over and over, "Do this!" or "Don't do that!" But children sometimes do not do what they are told. They may not understand, no matter how many times they are told; a mother should consider that the fault may lie with the words used to do the explaining. It is better to reconsider the method of presentation.

Language is imperfect. Words are incomplete. Therefore, it's not possible for them to be completely correct. There is no guarantee that imperfect words chosen by an imperfect speaker will be understood by the listener, who is himself imperfect as well.

EVEN THE KIND MAY BE DISLIKED

WORKING HARD is good, of course, but who is to say you are working correctly?

People often try very hard to maintain good relations with their spouses. If a person tells me, "I did everything I could for my wife, but still she left me," I ask, "Are you sure you did everything right? If you look inside yourself, you may find that you did not do everything you should have." Once a person realizes and accepts that, he can begin to feel, "I did my best, but it still didn't turn out the way that I had hoped. But, after all, both my spouse and I are imperfect. Because I did my best, I have no regrets."

HARD WORK DOES NOT GUARANTEE RESULTS

TRYING ONE'S HARDEST is not a bad thing; in fact, it's a good thing. But it's a mistake to expect that this will produce perfect results.

Such expectations are born from deep ignorance. The world cares nothing for your hopes, and it is perfect folly to expect that things will go your way. It's better to let go of such hopes and expectations entirely. The secret to a calm and happy life is to realize and accept that we are not perfect, and that we cannot expect others to be so. And because none of us is perfect, it is impossible to expect things to go perfectly well.

This does not mean that one should just give up trying. The wise and right way to live is to approach life with the attitude "I will do my best, without expecting something great to come from it." There is no space for anger in such a life. On the other hand, when people go about convinced of their own rightness or infallibility, they become angry when things don't go their way, and ultimately they meet with misfortune. How unwise.

HOW ANGRY PEOPLE THINK

THE SOURCE OF ANGER is something you should think seriously and deeply about. If you treat it as something trivial, it cannot help you find your way to joy.

In verse 3 from the Dhammapada (which means "the verses of the Dharma"), an ancient collection of the Buddha's words, we can see how angry people think:

> Akkocchi maṃ avadhi maṃ, ajini maṃ ahāsi me;
> Ye ca taṃ upanayhanti, veraṃ tesaṃ na sammati.

> He abused me, he struck me, he overpowered me;
> in those who harbor such thoughts hatred will never cease.

Let me annotate the important words of this verse. *Akkocchi* means "to abuse using strong language," and *maṃ* means "me." Similarly, *avadhi* means "to hurt or harm," which can be either in the physical or psychological sense. And in the final two phrases of the first line, *ajini* means "to defeat," and *ahāsi* means "to steal."

Such thoughts—of having been abused, harmed, stolen from, or defeated—are the source of anger.

ABUSE LEADS TO ANGER

THE PHRASE *akkocchi maṃ* indicates the sense that the world is teasing or mocking you. When people hear others talk, they sometimes think, "Those people are making fun of me" or "They're ignoring me" or "They're calling me names." Does this feel good? Of course not. It feels bad and can lead to anger.

People remember these emotions for a long time. They quickly forget things they studied hard to learn but carry insults with them forever. This is how we humans are—we forget the things that might help us, but we remember negative experiences for our whole lives.

Only when something bad happens does our memory work so well.

HARM LEADS TO ANGER

IN THE SECOND PHRASE, *avadhi maṃ*, the speaker says, "They have harmed me." In life, people do all kinds of harm and violence to each other. In school, for instance, some children may physically bully others. But bullying does not end with childhood and is not limited to a single gender. Men and women do things to hurt others, and the victims never forget that they were hurt.

This is human nature. We forget truly important things quickly but remember negative ones as if they are etched in stone. Complacently giving in to that tendency amplifies suffering.

DEFEAT LEADS TO ANGER

IN *AJINI MAṂ* the speaker cries, "They defeated me." The world is a competitive place, which means that there will always be both winners and losers. In business, sometimes we gain, and sometimes we lose. In school entrance exams and job interviews as well, some will be chosen while others will fail to pass. There is always someone who doesn't come out on top.

We all need to get used to the idea of losing, for if we cannot accept this, our worlds will be filled with sorrow and grief. Life itself is based on struggle; when something succeeds it inevitably means that somewhere, something has been defeated. This is a simple truth, like watching a race between children at school. One will come in first; another will come in last. That is reality.

The reason that a person wins is due to his or her talents and abilities. If you do not have the same level of ability, then it's natural that you will lose. There is not much else to say about it. But the loser often thinks, "If that other person wasn't there, I would have passed the test," or "If it hadn't been for him, I would have gotten the job I wanted." For example, there are times when two women both love the same man. But he cannot marry both, so he chooses only one of them. When this happens, the woman who was not chosen may become jealous, spiteful, or enraged. I occasionally meet such people myself. A woman may complain, "That other woman used all kinds of tricks to steal the man away from me, even though I love him more than she does." Ultimately, no matter the specifics of the situation, the result is anger.

People are strange. They always think about competing and getting ahead, but when they lose, they feel unhappy. Why feel bad about losing? If you are going to compete, there is definitely going to be a loser, just as there will be a winner. It would be best to accept either outcome with the same equanimity. But people do not, and when they lose, they get angry.

THEFT LEADS TO ANGER

THE MEANING of *ahāsi me* is "they stole from me." This is a frequent occurrence; people trick others out of their money by deceit, or businesses use unethical practices to win contracts. For the person who feels he has been stolen from, just as with those who feel abused, or harmed, or beaten, the reaction is one of anger.

ADULTS BROOD ON NEGATIVES AND AGGRAVATE SITUATIONS

WHEN A BABY sees a flower, he's happy; when scolded by his mother, he's sad. Babies don't dwell on bad experiences from the past. I think it would be wonderful if everyone could find this purity in their own hearts. But adults are different. They remember bad experiences all too well, calling them to mind and revisiting how they felt over and over. Once this cycle begins, what do you think is the result?

> Ye ca taṃ upanayhanti, veraṃ tesaṃ na sammati.
>
> In those who harbor such thoughts, hatred will never cease.

Essentially, it's as if someone brooded, "They abused me, aggrieved me, and caused me hurt. They beat me and stole from me," over and over again, as if his or her mind concocted these thoughts endlessly and vividly. That is how the minds of people with penchants for negative emotions function. They brood: "I lost" or "I wish things had turned out better."

This kind of thinking gives rise to anger. The emotion grows and grows, and even before it hurts others, it begins to destroy the individual himself. It can bring only misfortune.

THE EGO ENGENDERS ANGER

THE EGO, the notion of self, causes this ridiculous rumination on past hurts.

People can use terms like *I*, *we*, *me*, *mine*, or *self* without any harm in the conventional sense. However, people prefer to give substantial value to these harmless words and assume that some unchanging entity called "I," "me," or "self" exists. People emotionally attach themselves to these concepts and consider them to be distinct, important, and unique beings. This is the dearly held concept of ego. The ego's vain thinking, such as "I should be this way," or "I'm great," or "People should respect me," is the source of anger—and a great obstacle to joy.

Thinking very strongly "I'm a man" leads to prejudice about women as "others" and vice versa. Thinking "I studied hard and went to a good university" can lead to the idea that those who did not are somehow beneath you. Ego-centered emotions, feelings, and thoughts change one into a genuine fool.

No matter how great or accomplished you might be, if you belittle or ignore others, you will have difficulty in your relationships. The situation won't improve until you change.

EGO → IGNORANCE → CORRUPTION → ANGER

PEOPLE MAY HOLD ideas about themselves such as being a man, or young, or old, or someone's boss, but none of these roles is really so important. So what if you are the president of a company?

Believing that the self is rigidly defined is the source of all the world's problems. If people would only let go of these beliefs, the problems would vanish as well. Ego is nothing but an impediment to joy. It is an illusion.

In Buddhism, the most important thing is whether a person is doing the right thing, not whether they happen to be a housewife, a monk, or a CEO. The only question that matters is whether a person's behavior is right or wrong. If a young child happens to say the right thing, people should respect that, regardless of the age of the child or social conventions about whether children should speak up. Disregarding a child who speaks rightly is simply ignorant.

When thinking about the problem of anger, ego is the single most important concern. Once an ego has been formed, it tends to accumulate all kinds of garbage around it, making it ever more difficult to clear away. The ego gives rise to ignorance, and ignorance leads to corruption. And once corruption has set in, it can transform to anger when it is threatened.

ANGER IS HABIT-FORMING

ANGRY PEOPLE feel as if enemies surround them. This is due to the ego. Because they cling to concepts about themselves, about being one gender or another, or a member of some political party or religion, they become angry when another person disturbs that self-image in some way.

Once the anger reaction becomes routine, it can be very difficult to break out of.

People believe things about themselves, about their roles in life and their places in the world, without giving them much thought, but who really decides these things? This is only the ignorance born of ego.

II

ANGER DESTROYS HAPPINESS

WHEN REJECTION GROWS TOO STRONG

ANGER ARISES when we see, hear, taste, smell, or think about something that we reject out of a sense of distaste or dislike; the energy that accompanies feelings such as "I don't want to eat that" or "I can't stand talking to that person" is anger. When this rejection energy grows strong, it can be a terrible thing. The feeling of not wanting to talk to or encounter some person can easily evolve into the feeling of not even wanting that person to exist. If it escalates even further, the feeling can become so strong that it becomes impossible even to tolerate the person living in the same country—you may even want to kill him.

That's how far anger can go—to the point where it's capable of tearing apart nature, society, anything in its path. But we also know that anger is born from within, so we can say this much about it: "If you fix yourself, you can leave anger behind." In truth, it's entirely up to you.

IS ANGER UNAVOIDABLE?

MANY PEOPLE tell me, "Anger is a natural feeling. Doesn't that mean it's normal to get angry?"

Just as we discussed earlier: you might see a flower and think it's pretty, and you may feel it's natural to be disgusted when you see a cockroach. You might see some slice of roast pork on a tray and think it looks delicious but feel distaste at seeing a dead snake that has been cut into pieces. Many people would say that such reactions are commonsense or obvious. Such reactions are actually relative and personal; nothing is intrinsically attractive or repulsive.

Still, you might be thinking that these are natural feelings. Anger is just as natural as love; they are both part of being human. Most people give in at that point in their thinking; they stop trying to escape from anger, thinking, "I guess I just have a short temper. And anyway, it's only natural to get angry sometimes."

Believing that anger is a normal, natural human emotion is undeniably one way of thinking about it. But doing so eliminates the aspiration for further effort. Complacency with anger can be dangerous. It's the same as shrugging your shoulders and giving up. But where does giving up lead you?

ANGER ELIMINATES THE HAPPINESS
OF LIVING

WHAT IS an angry person's life like? I explained before that the birth of anger means the loss of happiness. This means that a person who is continually angry can feel no joy. Such people live pitiful lives full of complaint and woe. That's a pity, isn't it? If a person feels that anger is natural, then he or she might accept such a joyless, woeful condition as also a natural part of his or her personality—and so inescapable—but such a life seems sorrowful nonetheless.

Humans are capable of finding happiness in their lives, experiencing the joys of working, of raising children, of doing one's best, and of being with others. The joys of living. There are also more ephemeral joys and pleasures, such as those that come from eating a delicious meal while traveling or even wearing nice clothes. But people who are constantly angry lose their ability to enjoy any of these things.

Try dining or going on a trip with a constantly angry person. Doubtless he will find much to complain about and nothing to enjoy. People who are unable to take pleasure in the world around them are unable to feel happy about anything, even things that others generally enjoy. How sad. Furthermore, angry people steal the happiness of others who accompany them. So dismissing anger as a "natural" part of the human condition does not make sense; everybody seeks happiness and anger annihilates happiness.

PEOPLE CANNOT LIVE WITHOUT HAPPINESS

EVEN A DROP of rain is welcome in a dry season. Human happiness is the same.

Just keeping our bodies in good shape can be hard enough, let alone facing the other struggles and sufferings of life. Any happiness is a blessing like a drop of water in a drought. Work may be hard, but there can still be moments of satisfaction, gladness, and when things go well, achievement. Raising children is no easy thing, but there are moments of love, adoration, and happiness at watching them grow. Such pleasures are what make life worth living.

THERE IS NO SUCH THING AS
JUSTIFIABLE ANGER

IGNORING ANGER has consequences for us all. If we fail to control anger, how can anyone be happy?

We must never be complacent in the face of this problem, but rather he should strive to change our personalities so that anger is never born. This does not mean, however, that we should fight against anger, for that struggle is only another form of anger. Instead, it means cultivating one's personality so that anger never arises.

One path—popular in books and movies—to becoming recognized as a hero or a force for good is by doing battle with wrongdoers. But what is needed to fight against and defeat such people? Anger. This means that beneath the mask of heroism lies an attempt to normalize anger. Indeed, heroes that go out in search of villains to conquer are simply embodiments of this negative emotion. Even people who are not considered heroes but have powerful senses of fighting against something in their lives suffer great stress and cause many problems for others. Even the process of learning, which is usually quite enjoyable, can become a source of anger if you are troubled by too strong a desire to score well on a test, to gain entrance to a particular school, or to do better than a rival in your class.

There is no such thing as justifiable anger; it cannot be rationalized. We may frequently hear that anger is the obvious response to some situation or other, but there's nothing obvious about it at all.

KILLING CAN NEVER BE RIGHT

IN MAHAYANA BUDDHISM, there's a concept of compassionate righteousness practiced by enlightened beings called *bodhisattvas*. These are individuals who forgo their own salvation in order to first help save others: in modern language, what we would call heroes. But let us think for a moment what a bodhisattva's actions might be. Would a bodhisattva think, "I'll rid the world of wrongdoers, for there is much evil in the world"? Of course not—a bodhisattva has vowed to save *all* beings, including the "wrongdoers."

Instead of thinking, "How many people do I need to kill in order to cleanse the world of evil? I may need to kill every living human," wouldn't it be faster just to try to change oneself so that the desire to defeat or slay evil is abolished from your mind?

Everyone is liable to feel that the death of a bad person is no loss. But if every person who did something wrong were to be done away with, how many would death have to take? Wouldn't that mean the end of humanity? None of us is perfectly good, so the idea that only the good should live, while the bad should perish, is dangerous.

FORGIVE EVERYTHING

ONE DAY, Jesus Christ came upon a crowd of people who had caught an adulteress and were preparing to stone her to death—the punishment for adultery. They had tied her to a post and had gathered a pile of stones, but Jesus asked them what they were doing. They told him, "This woman is an adulteress who has betrayed her husband. According to God's law, we must stone her." Jesus replied, "I see. Then let he who has not sinned cast the first stone." On hearing that, none was able to pick up a stone, and the woman's life was spared.

Jesus spoke the truth. It's strange to think that it's natural or right to punish those who have done wrong. There is nothing that makes it all right to kill.

Jesus was encouraging forgiveness, complete and without limits. This is the correct way and the path to happiness, to carrying the kingdom of God within you. In Christianity, this is called *godliness*. There are other words for it in other religions. The word itself is not terribly significant; forgiveness is what is important. In Buddhism, we simply say, "Be compassionate, and forgive."

ANGER IS A CONSUMING FIRE

ANGER HAS MANY negative consequences.

I have already explained how anger leads to unhappiness. That is easy enough to understand; being angry doesn't feel good. People are unhappy when they carry anger inside. When you're free of anger, the opposite is true—your heart feels light and clear. It's a wonderful feeling; it's what we know as *happiness*.

Love is the energy of creation, of building and raising things, while anger is the negative energy of rejection and destructiveness. Where does anger begin? Within your own body, and it begins to destroy the body from the instant it's born.

If your body were aflame, you would burn whatever you touched. But what would happen even before that? You would burn yourself. In this sense, anger is like fire, which has the power to destroy other things but starts by destroying its original source. You may want to set fire to a pile of trash, but it is the match that is consumed by the fire first. You may not want it to be destroyed, as matches can be useful, but it's hopeless to think that it will set the trash alight without first catching flame itself.

ANGER IS INSIDIOUS IN ITS HARM

As we can see, becoming angry is like setting fire to oneself. Your body immediately begins to feel the effects right down to each individual cell. To see how this works, take a fresh vegetable and expose it to heat. The succulent leaf or stalk will begin to wither right away. The same kind of thing happens in the body when it holds anger.

Of course, if we felt a burning pain in our hands, or were crippled, or felt sick to our stomachs the instant we began to feel angry, we would avoid doing so. But anger gives no such warning signs, which makes it even more frightening than fire.

Our hearts, lungs, and kidneys—all of our organs—must work twenty-four hours every day. If our bodies are overloaded by anger, we tax them even further. People who get angry and complain a lot can develop serious ailments such as sleeplessness, high blood pressure, ulcers, or chronic pain.

ANGRY PEOPLE CAN BE SLOW
TO RECOVER FROM SICKNESS

You may have noticed that when positive, easygoing people get sick, they quickly make friends with the people taking care of them; this can lead to more effective treatment and a speedier recovery. When patients are cheerful, the nurses enjoy their work more and do their best to help them get well as soon as possible.

But some patients are the opposite, always finding things to complain about. The nurses may roll their eyes whenever they are called into the room, only to find out that the patient just wants a blanket adjusted, or a cup moved to a slightly different spot on his bedside table. Such behavior only interferes with the nurses' real work, but the patient persists in this wrong-headed sense of entitlement.

Which of these do you think will recover more slowly? The angry people, of course. And the longer they stay in the hospital, the more they will upset those around them, until no one will want even to enter their room. Doctors and nurses may struggle with thinking, "What a pain in the neck!" as they do their jobs, and it will be harder for them to develop any kind of empathy or rapport. In the end, this only leads to a worsening of the patient's condition—and more suffering.

ANGRY PEOPLE ARE THIEVES OF JOY

IF ANGRY PEOPLE were the only ones to be negatively affected by their anger, perhaps it would be fine just to leave them to it, even to let them destroy themselves. But in fact angry people cause great problems for those around them as well. No matter how hard you're working to achieve happiness, an angry person can steal it away in a moment. They are the thieves of joy.

Ordinary thieves simply steal things, which is not so terrible. If someone ate some food you'd prepared for yourself, after all, this would probably not be enough to make you truly angry. And if the culprit later said, "Hey, that was really good! Could you make it again?" you might even feel pleased and think, "Well, even if I lost a little pleasure, it's nice to see someone so happy." Praise and gratitude can be a wonderful substitute for what was lost. So we can see that much depends on the manner of stealing being done; not every thief takes away happiness.

But angry people take from us the most important thing in life. The rob us of our very reason for living. Someone who steals money has the clear objective of using another person's wealth to make his own life easier. But angry people who steal happiness from others do not become happy because of it. They suffer from their anger as well. They destroy others' happiness and engulf them in their rage. For this reason, the angry are the worst thieves of all.

ANGER IS INFECTIOUS

WE HUMANS—and our emotions—are easily influenced by our environments. Take, for example, what happens when a child sees something she wants, but her mother refuses to buy it. She may throw a tantrum and attack her mother, but if someone distracts her and says something funny, the child will stop crying and start laughing almost immediately, soon forgetting that she was crying at all.

This is true for all people, not just children. Our moods are strongly affected by our surroundings.

We also match our emotions to others around us. Try bringing just one angry person into a group of people that had been enjoying themselves. What do you think will happen? The mood will darken instantaneously. If someone walks into a party, where forty young people are dancing and having fun, and begins to yell at everyone, what will the effect be? A single person erasing forty people's happiness.

You need to think about this if you want to understand anger. An angry person has something like a demon within him, which radiates a terrible power out in all directions, destroying not only his own but everyone else's happiness—even that of the society in which he lives.

IT'S DANGEROUS FOR ONE PERSON
TO BE IN CONTROL OF OTHERS

SOMETIMES WHEN the leaders of a country become angered, they start a war. When that happens, other innocent people with nothing to be angry about are forced to go fight and die. History is full of tales of such foolish leaders, with bad hearts and little understanding or ability. The desire to be in charge, to be king, or to control other people is itself foolish. Wise people have no interest in doing so. And because it's impossible to know when such a person—an unintelligent person in a position of authority—will become maddened and enraged, that person represents a real danger.

For that reason, there need to be controls over those who are in positions of power. In the United States, for example, there are many people who have some control over the president. Checks and balances have been put in place to mitigate the risk of leaving all decisions to a single man. The president is surrounded by knowledgeable advisors to support and guide him. Without such control systems in place, there's no telling what might happen.

Avoiding anger is a personal issue, but it is also something that must be done for the sake of all living beings.

A WINNER DOESN'T ACTUALLY WIN

VERSE 6 of the Dhammapada:

> Pare ca na vijānanti, mayamettha yamāmase;
> Ye ca tattha vijānanti, tato sammanti medhagā.

> Other people (the unwise) do not realize that all in
>   this world must die;
> The wise recognize this, and cease in their vying.

The reason there is conflict in the world is because there are people who do not understand that their fighting will lead to their own destruction and death. Their great error is that they ignore the damage that they have taken and focus only on having defeated their rivals. We see this, for example, when someone says, "Everybody else is afraid to speak up to that guy, but I just gave him a piece of my mind. That'll teach him to mess with me."

But this is only self-deception. When you get angry at another, you must first experience negative feelings that only do damage to yourself. But angry people do not see this. When people truly understand that anger is self-destructive, they do not become angry no matter what happens. No matter how bad a situation or how difficult a job or how strong language they might be forced to endure, they do not anger. They know that to do so would only hurt themselves.

Think of getting angry as you would of drinking poison. There is no reason for you to do this to yourself, is there? In order to stop becoming angry, you need to understand that it's destructive to you.

BECOMING ANGRY IS FOOLISH

THERE IS NOTHING in the world more foolish than an angry person. This is the objective truth, not a joke. The angry are so stupid it's embarrassing.

Look inside yourself when you get angry. You lose your intelligence, the brightness within you. People in that state are neither human nor beast. They're lower than animals. If you want to be a person with normal intelligence, ability, and talents, you must never become angry. Feelings rise and fall like waves in our minds, but if you look back on your own life, you should recognize that those times that you used your head and clearly understood what was around you were times when you were not angry.

You should remind yourself frequently that getting angry is a foolish thing to do. Drill it into your head that only the foolish allow anger to overcome them. If you begin getting angry, tell yourself the truth: "I'm being an irrational fool, ignorant and uncomprehending."

When someone does something wrong, you don't feel angry if you understand both why the person made the mistake and what you can say to help him or her avoid it in the future. You can deal with it calmly, without becoming disappointed or upset. When you are able to use your wisdom, you will not become angry.

STAY ANGRY, AND YOU WILL
BECOME ANGER

WHEN WE BECOME angry, at that moment we are the worst form of ignorant fool. And the anger triggers even further ignorance, perpetuating itself and making things even worse. So what happens when people get angry more frequently?

An odd thing about the human mind is that repetition leads to belief. If people are constantly told a thing is good, they will decide that it is good. Humans participate in a kind of mutual mind control; each person influences others.

Anger works the same way. The more a person gets angry, the more they *become* anger. Such a person is more akin to a walking heap of meat than to a human—and just as frightening. If you were alone one night and encountered some monster with a single eye in its bloody face and teeth sticking out everywhere, you'd be afraid, wouldn't you? You wouldn't want to see such a thing. Of course, such monsters are no more than fantasies and illusions. But if you meet up with a walking, talking mass of flesh that has lost its humanity, that is truly frightening.

DON'T THROW AWAY YOUR HUMANITY

TO BECOME ANGRY is to throw away your humanity. You have no further hope of growth or development so long as you remain in that state.

People who are able to let go of their egos and leave anger behind can truly be happy.

III

THOSE WHO DON'T GET ANGRY

RESPONDING TO ANGRY PEOPLE

PEOPLE MAY BE curious about how Buddhists handle a person who becomes unruly at a temple. Of course we do not beat them or yell at them. Getting upset at a person, and berating or scolding him or her, is itself just another form of angry behavior.

Frequently, what we do is ignore the offender completely. This is a form of total social isolation, ignoring everything a person does and says. It doesn't mean physically exiling such people; in fact, it's fine even to have meals with them. They are human beings, after all, so we would not deprive such people of food, and if they were to become ill, we would care for them. But otherwise the punishment involves completely ignoring them, passing right over them in conversations as if they weren't there. This has an extremely powerful impact. Most people cannot bear the stress of having their very existence negated.

The kinds of people who are subject to this treatment include those who act immorally, those who refuse to work with others, those who disregard social conventions, and selfish people who constantly bully or tease others. In ignoring such people, the message is "You are free to continue acting that way, but so long as you do, you will never be accepted in our society." It's as if they are not there at all. For the subject of the punishment, this is very difficult to bear. And the treatment continues until the culprit acknowledges the error of his or her ways and makes an apology.

THE DRIVER WHO TROUBLED
THE BUDDHA

BEFORE HE LEFT home, Siddhartha Gotama was a royal prince, and he had a carriage driver and groom named Channa. Channa thought very highly of Siddhartha and did his best to take care of him. When Siddhartha first left home to become a spiritual seeker, Channa was his only companion. By then, Siddhartha no longer rode in a carriage, instead riding a horse, but because Channa had always accompanied and watched over his master, he didn't leave his side. After traveling far from their homes, Siddhartha entrusted Channa with a great responsibility; he gave Channa his royal crown and jewels and robes and told him to go back to his father, the king, and tell him that his son had left home to take up the spiritual path.

Channa later also left home to follow the Buddhist path, but he soon found that his relationship with Siddhartha Gotama (the Buddha) was completely different than it had been before. Where once he had always been the closest person to Siddhartha, he now found that he was never able to get near him, for the Buddha was surrounded by many monks. The great *arahants* (fully enlightened individuals) such as Sariputta, Moggallana, and Maha Kassapa were now always by the Buddha's side, and he would speak to them and ask them to perform various services for him.

Leaving the world to follow the path of Buddhism means entering a sacred realm in which the highest priority is on moral behavior, rather than birth, wealth, or relationships. For this reason, those closest to the Buddha were the pure and the enlightened, while others, including Channa, were left to work on their spiritual practice and were unable to be as near to him.

Since the Buddha no longer relied on him for his service, Channa became lonely and began to complain. "What do all of you think you're doing? Now that he has become famous and a great man, you flock to his side. But who has been taking care of him since he was a little boy? Who accompanied him when he first left home? Isn't it I that has always looked after him?" In this way, Channa began to try to lord it over the other monks, and he would not listen to what anyone said. People would try to tell him what was expected of followers of the path, or how to do some particular thing, but he would only scold and rebuff them in a fearsome way. This made it difficult for everyone to practice, as well as making it impossible to teach Channa anything at all. The only one Channa never complained to was the Buddha himself. He did not say anything to him at all about how he felt.

The disciples were concerned and wondered what to do about this. And the Buddha himself was very troubled. He cared very deeply about others and felt enormous gratitude and obligation to those who had cared for him. He knew that Channa thought the world of him, and that he would have given his own life for the Buddha's, so he was deeply concerned that his behavior meant that he would never find enlightenment.

BRAHMA DANDA,
THE BUDDHA'S DISCIPLINE

So just before he died, the Buddha made a request of his disciple Ananda. "Channa has been behaving very selfishly and refusing to listen to what anyone says. This worries me, so I want you and all the others to practice *brahma danda* with him when I am gone." *Brahma* means "great" or "holy," while *danda* means "punishment." Together, they mean "the punishment meted out by the holy."

Of course, holy men do not beat or strike others. In fact, the words seemed to be a contradiction in terms, so Ananda asked, "What is this brahma danda?" The Buddha replied, "All bhikkhus of the community should approve a rule by consensus to ignore Channa. Channa may speak to monks. However none of the members of the community should ever respond to him. And he must be informed that this is to be his punishment." This is brahma danda: all of the members of a group ignore one member completely.

There is a form of bullying that children do in which they all ignore a member of their class. Buddhism does not suggest that this form of abuse is appropriate. Brahma danda is a formal punishment that is decided upon in a council by the members of the Buddhist community. The person who is to be punished is notified of the decision and the form it will take. Children, on the other hand, do not decide to ignore someone at a student council meeting; they just decide to shut out some child they do not like. This is wrong. In Japan, the law provides for punishments such as arresting and imprisoning those who break laws, but individuals and groups do not have the authority to do so. Similarly, while the Buddhist community may elect to use this punishment, children in a school or people working in an office should not.

In the tumultuous days after the Buddha's *parinirvana*, or death, once the funeral proceedings had been completed, the monks decided to enforce his will. The council met and ruled that they would all begin to ignore Channa, as the Buddha had decreed. Ordinarily, they would have called him to the council meeting as well, but in this case they did not. Instead, Ananda later went to Channa's room and informed him of the decision. They had both known the Buddha since boyhood, so doubtless they were both grieving his loss.

Ananda said, "The Buddha decided your punishment before his parinirvana."

"What is it to be?" asked Channa.

"Brahma danda, the punishment of holy men."

"What is that?" Channa asked.

"From this day, all of us will ignore anything you say. You, however, are free to talk."

Channa fainted at hearing these words. That is how great the impact of the punishment was on him. But we should not change or soften a decision just because it's hard on a person. And in fact, after receiving this great shock, Channa began to practice in earnest, and he reached enlightenment soon thereafter. At the moment he attained enlightenment, his punishment was nullified. However he still fulfilled his moral obligation by seeking forgiveness, saying, "I have caused much trouble to the Buddha, but I vow to control myself in the future, so I ask for your pardon and for all punishments to be raised." The community held another council and decided that they would accept Channa's apology and admit him back into the group.

THE IMPORTANCE OF
SELF-REFLECTION

THERE ARE PEOPLE who act in ways that are grossly unacceptable to society, and if no one were to admonish or punish them, they might only be emboldened, and their behavior would worsen. In this sense, anger has a place; the fear of righteous anger can serve to suppress such misbehavior, and this is provided for in our legal systems. In law, however, it isn't referred to as *anger*, but as *punishment*, and it generally involves the deprivation of personal liberty for a specified time. Many people exercise self-control and obey laws because they fear the wrath of the law and the loss of freedom.

This definition of anger applies only to the legal system; people as individuals should not take enforcing the law into their hands. A system cannot get truly "angry" in the sense we're discussing in this book—only individuals. Anger is a destructive force of the mind.

In Buddhism, there is no concept of becoming angry with people for their misdeeds. That said, there are appropriate punishments for those who might mistakenly think that this absence of anger gives them a license to do whatever they wish: brahma danda, for instance.

One metaphor for the cultivation of a Buddhist is "to show him a mirror." This means to teach someone who does bad things to look at his or her own behavior objectively. Such people are told to "look in the mirror"; Buddhist monks are constantly engaged in this kind of self-observation, always checking whether or not they're conducting themselves properly. Without this self-reflection, the rest of spiritual practice is meaningless, for without it, fixing error is impossible. People who want to improve themselves should think about how willing they are to look objectively at what they have done.

Simply put, avoiding anger is not a simple decision on the part of a weak personality—one must be honest and strong.

COMING TO UNDERSTAND YOUR WRONGS

IN JAPANESE MYTH, there is a deity named Emma who sits in judgment of the dead, deciding who will go to heaven and who to hell. His means of judging the dead is different from that in Western religions; he doesn't simply filter believers to one side and nonbelievers to another. Instead, Emma simply instructs dead souls to stand in front of a mirror. There they see reflected everything they did when they were alive—and recognize by themselves whether it was good or bad. A person may realize, for instance, "I have done nothing but wrong," and prepare to be sent to hell. A soul's relegation to hell is not Emma's responsibility. Even if Emma does nothing, the soul understands and accepts its destination.

This is not a story about punishment, about returning evil for evil, or wrong for wrong, but rather it is about the acknowledgment and acceptance of those wrongs that you have done. The next time someone is judging you too harshly, instead of fighting back or judging him in return, it might be more effective just to "show him a mirror." That is the simplest way to get people to change.

IF SOMEONE STRIKES YOU...

THE MONK SARIPUTTA was famous for his placid, humble nature. In fact, the Buddha always referred to him as "my right hand" and even wondered aloud whether he, the Buddha, or Sariputta was the best model for disciples to emulate. That is how highly he praised this monk. Sariputta was blessed with profound wisdom and uncommon knowledge, but at the same time he was the humblest man alive. He was so self-effacing, in fact, that people would unknowingly ask him, "Who is this great Sariputta?"

One day a man of the high Brahmin caste heard that Sariputta was deeply wise, but when he saw him, he said, "What? He's just some old bald guy!" Then he thought, "We'll see how great he really is!" and he ran after Sariputta when he was setting out to collect alms and struck him very hard from behind.

Now, when people are struck out of the blue, some kind of reaction is normal and expected, but Sariputta did not even turn around. He just kept walking slowly on his way. The Brahmin, who had been anticipating some kind of response, was awestruck at Sariputta's imperturbability and decided to keep following him. But Sariputta never once looked his way. Only then did the man realize what a terrible thing he had done. He thought, "This man truly is great, and I did something despicable to him," and he became very afraid, trembling and breaking into a cold sweat. He ran in front of Sariputta, dropped to his knees, and begged forgiveness for his action.

But when he did, Sariputta only looked down at him and said, "Forgive you for what? What have you done?" That is how little concern he showed at having been struck. He did not even wonder whether the man might have been the one who had hit him a little while earlier. With that, the Brahmin was even more deeply impressed by Sariputta's tremendous self-possession and grew even more afraid.

He admitted to Sariputta, "I have done a great wrong. It was I that struck you." Sariputta replied, "Ah, it was nothing to me. I forgive you." And following this exchange, the Brahmin became a convert to Buddhism.

GREAT PEOPLE ARE HUMBLE

WE WOULD BE able to avoid anger, just like Sariputta, if only we could let go of senseless pride.

One time, the tiniest section of Sariputta's robe was hanging down out of place. A young novice of the order noticed and said to him, "Excuse me, but look at your robe." At which Sariputta immediately bowed down and said, "Oh, thank you very much for telling me." This novice was just a boy, practicing under the tutelage of noble Sariputta, and Sariputta was the Buddha's own right hand, but he had no sense of ego about this; when the acolyte told him of his error, all he felt was gratitude.

We may not be able to emulate this perfectly, but I think it's a wonderful lesson to keep in mind. Becoming angry due to an egoistic sense of "But I'm the boss" or "Because I'm right" is only a very ugly form of selfishness. Please remember that. This is why humility is so important. To Buddhists, Buddha was the greatest person ever to have lived, and Sariputta was a close second. But when someone told this great man that his hem was out of place, he simply thanked him. And so it should be.

SELF-IMAGE IS UGLINESS

ALL TOO OFTEN our attitude is expressed in words such as "Just who do you think you are?" or "Don't act out of place." In schools as well, younger students who speak up to upperclassmen are often shouted down. This is true at all grade levels—the older students will always strike out if a younger one says something they don't like.

This is ugly. In Japan, subordinates are expected to tolerate any and all abuse their seniors dish out—verbal or physical. They can't even complain if they are treated as virtual slaves, even being forced to wash their seniors' underwear. If they voice any opinions whatsoever, they are shouted at to keep quiet and know their place.

But is this really enjoyable for the senior group? I hardly think so. This kind of hierarchical system is bad for both the upper and the lower group. They all suffer under it. This is why truly great people never tell others to "know their place." If someone lets them know they made a mistake, they just admit and accept it. Even if a young boy tells them they did something wrong, they praise him.

If a student points out a mistake a teacher has made, the correct response is to acknowledge the error and praise the student for her knowledge and maturity. That is a magnanimous reaction.

EINSTEIN'S HUMILITY

WHEN ALBERT EINSTEIN was a professor at Princeton, it happened that a local schoolteacher knew where he lived. One day, a young girl in his class was having difficulty with arithmetic, and he teasingly said to her, "Why can't you study harder? Did you know that right next door to where you live, there's a man who is very good at math?"

The little girl had no idea that he was talking about such a great man. She simply thought, "I see. Maybe the old man that lives next door can help me with my math homework," and after school she went and rang his doorbell. Einstein opened the door and, seeing the little girl standing there, invited her to come in. Once inside she told him, "My teacher said you're good at math. Could you help me with my homework?" Einstein was of course very busy, and was already considered something of a national treasure, but without hesitation, he agreed and sat down with her and helped with all of her homework problems.

Back at school, the teacher noticed that the little girl had gotten much better at arithmetic. Curious about the change, he said, "You seem to be doing much better now. What happened?"

She told him, "I just did what you said and asked the old man next door for help."

The teacher was shocked and after school called the girl's mother to explain what had happened. "I had no idea she would actually go to his house. I just meant to tell her that a great scientist was living right next door." Together, the teacher and the girl's mother went to Einstein's house to apologize for disturbing him. But when they did, Einstein replied, "Not at all. I didn't teach her anything. In fact, I learned quite a bit from her. I was the one fortunate enough to have such a teacher."

As we can see, the great are truly great. Einstein, who had developed the theory of relativity, was profoundly more knowledgeable than the little girl. Yet he admitted to having learned many things from her. It seems that the greater the person is, the more he is able to learn, even from a small child. A lesser person might have seen the little girl at the doorstep and huffed, "Go away. I'm much too busy to be bothered." But what then would he gain?

From this great man's humbleness, we can learn a means of curing ourselves of anger. The trick is to make the effort to become great oneself, to strive toward bigness of character, of spirit and heart, and even if one does not achieve greatness, to try to act as the great do.

SHED ANGER LIKE AN OLD SKIN

ONE OF THE MOST important texts in Buddhism is the Sutta Nipata; it's said that even Shakyamuni himself would refer back to it to cite things that he had previously said. I encourage all of you to read it if you have the opportunity.

There's a verse in the Sutta Nipata that essentially says, "When you feel anger arise, control it." The way to do this is the same as using medicine to control the spread of a poison. Essentially, one must treat anger like a poison; as soon as it's detected, use an antidote to rid oneself of it. In this case, the antidote is following and practicing in the Buddhist path.

The next part of the verse talks about how to rid oneself of anger, which it likens to a snake molting its skin. In Buddhism, anger is described as a lethal poison.

ONLY THOSE WHO DON'T BECOME
ANGRY PREVAIL

HERE I'D LIKE to talk about another passage from the Buddhist scriptures, verse 222 of the Dhammapada:

> Yo ve uppatitaṃ kodhaṃ, rathaṃ bhantaṃva vāraye;
> Tamahaṃ sārathiṃ brūmi, rasmiggāho itaro jano.

> Those who control fierce anger as it arises are like
>   those who can steer a runaway carriage.
> Others merely clutch at the reins.

Ordinary people only hold the reins; they do not have a professional charioteer's ability to control the carriage.

What does this mean, "to clutch at the reins?" A car that is breaking down often cannot be driven, but people with skill and technique may nevertheless be able to use it to reach their destination. Most people, however, would have no choice but to give up. In the Buddha's age of course there were no cars, only carriages, but these could also have problems, such as horses running out of control, or damaged wheels, yokes, or reins. A skilled driver would not have to give up just because one of these problems occurred; he would be able to get to where he was going.

Think of the carriage in the above metaphor as life. When anger arises, it's like an accident that threatens to send the carriage out of control. If a person continues to let anger run wild, it can become very dangerous, just as if a driver were to fail to control his horses. This is why anger needs to be checked the very moment it's born. People who are able to do this are skilled or accomplished; they are leaders and successful in life. The meaning here is that he who becomes angry loses; those who do not, prevail.

The word *sārathiṃ* means "driver," but it also carries the meanings "leader," "winner," and "hero." The idea is that true leaders and heroes are those who have learned to extirpate anger. People who are full of pride at their own greatness, or who belittle others, are not leaders.

The Buddha added emphasis to his words using the phrase *Tamahaṃ... brūmi*, which means "Thus say I..." He used this phrase to introduce statements that might be difficult for people to accept or which contravened conventional beliefs. The truths that he would emphasize in this way are nonetheless accessible to any person who seeks after them with an objective mind. Some things, however, can be more difficult to accept than others. For example, most people would agree that becoming angry with people who do bad things is normal and appropriate. But the Buddha said the opposite: that we simply should not become angry. Knowing this, the Buddha prefaced his statement with "Thus say I." The implication is "You may not agree with this, but it is the truth nonetheless." We need to understand that this phrase is used to introduce right paths, truths, the views of the Buddha that happened to be contrary to worldly opinion, and rules to be obeyed even if they were difficult to accept. "Those who do not become angry prevail" is such a statement.

Itaro jano means "other people," and *rasmiggāho* means "reins." People who cannot control anger and other emotions are like riders who clutch vainly at the reins without being able to use them. They have no skill as drivers. Even a child may be able to grasp the steering wheel of a car, but it takes study and practice to become licensed to drive. In Buddha's analogy, people who cannot control anger are like drivers whose hands only hold the wheel without steering. In contrast, those who control anger can steer not only their own car but other people's as well, which means the angry must follow where they lead.

Those who can control anger are always leaders. In politics, where there is all sorts of infighting, scheming, and personal attacks, the people who rise to the top positions are the ones who can smile and keep calm no matter what names people call them. That's the mark that distinguishes people in leadership positions. If someone became confrontational at the slightest prompting, she soon would be out of office. True leaders hold the reins and use them with skill.

BECOME LIKE A CRACKED BELL

THERE'S ANOTHER PASSAGE from the words of the Buddha, verse 221 of the Dhammapada, which I encourage you to remember:

Kodhaṃ jahe vippajaheyya mānaṃ.

Kodhaṃ jahe means "let go of anger," and *vippajaheyya mānaṃ* means "let go of pride, of the self." Rid yourself of anger and selfish pride. Having pride, having ego, is the source and cause of anger. Letting go is not an easy thing to do, but please keep in mind that this is what we should strive toward.

People become angry at inconsequential things. If another person simply walks in front of them, they may become irate, and so we all need to go around taking care not to offend anyone we happen to pass in front of, which is not such a bad thing, but requires some effort. The slightest mistake in manners can be taken as an affront. Even saying hello in the wrong way can make some people upset with you, like a bell that rings at the slightest touch. This is why the Buddha tells us to be like a cracked bell, which doesn't ring even when struck, no matter how hard. In the same way, no matter what happens, we should not become angry. This is the same as being free from self.

ANYONE CAN SEEM GREAT IF THEY HAVE NO CAUSE OF ANGER

THERE IS A famous story that illustrates the idea that anger is a dangerous and powerful poison of the mind.

There once was a monk who would consort with the nuns and was very friendly with them. Of course, leaving home and joining the Buddhist order is intended to make people independent and free from attachment; the formation of friendships and other personal relationships is not encouraged. So when this monk became close with the nuns, he was reprimanded.

The monk became angry at this, and the nuns, who thought that he was a good man, were angered at his treatment as well. Then, other monks, who saw how the nuns were behaving, themselves began to comment and ended up becoming angry as well. What a mess! When the Buddha was informed of the situation, he quickly chastised them all. Then, leaving the matter aside for a moment, he told the following story:

Not so long ago, in the town of Savatthi, a rich woman lived in a house along with her female servant. The rich woman had the reputation of being extremely patient and kind and of always keeping her temper. No one had ever seen her become angry or heard her raise her voice.

The servant thought to herself, "Everyone in town believes that my mistress is so calm and kindhearted. But I wonder if that is really true. Perhaps the reason she never gets angry is because I always do my job so well. I think I will see if she is truly as patient as everyone believes." And so one day, the servant overslept on purpose. She had been working in the same household for many, many years and never once had she made a mistake, and every day before her mistress arose, she would have finished her morning's chores and prepared breakfast. But on that day, her mistress awoke and found her still in bed. She went to the servant's room and asked, "Why are you still in bed?" And when the servant looked in her eyes, she saw that the lady of the house had become upset. "Oh, no special reason," she replied, and she got up and started her day's work.

The servant thought to herself, "Aha. So she does get angry. She just never had a reason before. Let's see what happens tomorrow." And so the next day she overslept again. The mistress came into her room and found her in bed and angrily shouted at her, "Get up! Why haven't you gotten out of bed yet?" "Oh, no special reason," said the servant.

"First she looked angry, then she scolded me," she thought. "I wonder what she will do next." And so the next day she stayed in bed again. The mistress was enraged and took a heavy wooden rod that was used to bar the door and struck the servant with it, opening a gash in her head so that she was soon covered in blood. Without saying a word to her, the servant ran outside and called out to everyone, "You all think that my mistress is such a patient, gentle woman, but look what she has done! And this is for only sleeping too late!" And in that single moment, the people of Savatthi began to whisper, "What a terrible woman. She loses her temper and mistreats her servants." And so the rich woman's reputation was ruined.

With this parable, the Buddha was teaching the message that anyone can be calm and avoid anger when there is no cause to be angry. A person may pretend to be calm, cool, and collected, but this is no more than a deception.

Sometimes people enter a temple for two or three weeks for retreats in which they can concentrate on their practice. When they finish, they may feel as if they have become better people, but this is not necessarily true. In order to find out if they have really become better, they need to go back out into the world. It's easy not to become angry when everyone around you is being nice, so avoiding anger in such circumstances is not a very impressive feat. If the conditions for causing anger later arise, perhaps you will become angry again. There is nothing particularly praiseworthy in not becoming angry when the conditions for anger are not in place.

A true lack of anger is only that which manifests even when all the conditions for causing anger are there—smiling even as the world abuses you.

REMAIN PEACEFUL, NO MATTER HOW YOU'RE TREATED

PEOPLE SCOLD others in many different ways, but the Buddha spoke of five different forms that scolding might be classified into:

1. There are times when scolding is justified and times when it is not.
2. Scolding may have a basis or may be baseless.
3. Scolding may be in gentle words or harsh.
4. Scolding may use meaningful, helpful words or words that are foolish and vain.
5. Scolding may be done out of compassion or simply out of anger.

Regardless of whether someone speaks to you with a basis for their words or none, uses gentle words or harsh, remain calm and try to maintain a bigness of heart. Regardless of whether they speak to you in anger, in compassion, or in jealousy, keep your heart and mind open. No matter what happens, remain peaceful and calm.

MAKE YOUR HEART UNMOVABLE

How does one cultivate a constantly peaceful mind? Think, for example, of a man who one day becomes angry at the earth—he takes a shovel, thinking, "I'll show this earth! I'll tear it apart! I'll destroy the whole thing!" But of course although a person with a shovel may dig a small hole, it has no real effect on the earth. What we should do is make our minds so imperturbable that when other people dig at us, we are as unmoved as the earth when it is picked at by a tiny shovel.

Or consider a person who tries to paint the sky with a brush. The person may think, "I'm going to paint the whole sky in all different colors!" but he will only succeed in getting his hands dirty. If you think of yourself as the sky, you can be as impossible to color by people's words. Whatever people say to you, let it fall away without staining your mind. Don't let people paint you with anger. Make it your goal never to be disturbed whether people speak to you kindly or in anger, or in any of the five ways the Buddha described.

There is another parable, which comes from India. In the old days, there were no flashlights, so people carried torches to guide them in the dark. What would happen if a person thought, "I am going to thrust this torch into the Ganges until the whole river boils away?" Of course, the river would flow on undisturbed, and the torch would be snuffed out. No matter what people may say to you, accept it like the Ganges, flowing calm and without care.

IV

THE SOLUTION TO ANGER

RECOGNIZE THE ANGER WITHIN YOURSELF

THE MANY BAD THINGS that people do—fighting, killing, attacking each other—are all done out of anger. Look at the world today. Somebody somewhere is angry and killing or trying to kill another person. People are humiliating and scorning others. Even entire countries are fighting against each other. This is no joke or exaggeration. A person who is angry can be like a beast or a demon. I'm sure that all of us know of someone who becomes like a monster when he is angry.

Now, if even a single occurrence of anger can be that scary, clearly becoming angry time and time again is even worse. There's nothing as terrible as anger that breeds more anger. You should tell yourself, "There is nothing as bad as becoming angry." And if you find yourself becoming angry, you should say, "Ah, I've sunk to the lowest level of life. I have to get out of this state right away," so that you can return to your humanity as soon as possible.

This does not mean using lots of energy to suppress anger; instead, when you see anger for what it really is, you will be unable to become angry at all. Please work toward this goal.

DO NOT REPRESS OR TOLERATE

ANGER IS NOT something that disappears if you try to hold it back. You may hear people talk about swallowing your anger, or trying to grin and bear it, but these cannot cause anger to cease. Anger is born from within, so no matter how much you grit your teeth, it will remain inside you. If you try to repress it, you'll have to keep on repressing for every moment until the day you die.

In the West, people are often told to find a method to vent their stress, to let it all out some way, like loosening a valve to release pent-up gas under pressure. But what could be more dangerous? For if we just talk about finding ways to release anger, this is no more than normalizing anger—treating the symptoms but ignoring the disease. If we accept this line of reasoning, then each time you happen to get angry, all you would need to do is to find another way of releasing it. But such outbursts inevitably cause problems for others, so there is nothing praiseworthy about them as a solution.

ANGER DISAPPEARS WHEN IT'S WATCHED

ANGER IS BORN from within the self, so the only means of disposing of it is by drawing it out, like a poison. In vipassanā meditation, this is known as being aware of the self in the here and now.

The moment anger arises, one should immediately look at it and observe it: "This is anger. This is how anger feels." Study the anger and learn from it. Say to yourself, "Right now, I am experiencing a negative feeling. This is how anger feels." Turn the eye that usually watches the outside world and use it to look within yourself.

At first you may notice how you become angry quickly at the slightest comment. But gradually people's words will affect you less as you learn to recognize and observe anger from the instant it arises. This observation extinguishes anger. Once anger is gone, you will feel better right away, just as when you take medicine for a headache and the pain goes away, like a fog lifting. The loss of anger has a similar effect—you will feel happier, clearer, and better as soon as it is gone.

Once you are able to do this, you will gain confidence in your own self-control and your mastery over anger, which is a true achievement. Once you are able to see anger as it arises, you will become able to listen to whatever other people may say, calmly and without being disturbed. It is a simple and instant effect. You do not need to do much, and there is no need for a grasp of psychology. Remember, all that you need to do is to watch inside yourself.

In my Buddhist practice, people who are not aware of themselves in the here and now are referred to in terms that mean "fools," "the dead," or "the sleeping." People who are not aware of anger as it arises become anger's demons. Even after their initial rage, they continue to look back in anger, often for many years, becoming upset every time they recall an incident, and each time doing further damage to themselves.

ANGER IS A LOSING REACTION

IN THIS SECTION, I'm going to talk about real methods for curing oneself of anger, but first I should make one important point clear, even though it may sound harsh: Everyone who gets angry does so out of a lack of self-confidence and a failure of character. It reveals the weakness and foolishness of a person who is afraid to show his lack of depth and tries to hide it behind a scary mask, howling like a beaten mongrel. It's all pretense and vanity.

There are even those in high social positions who still become angry with or scold those beneath them severely. Such people are devoid of true humanity. They become angry out of their great ignorance, and of course they cannot be considered to be leaders in any true sense. So please remember this: the angry are no more than those who have been defeated by the world.

ANGRY PARENTS AREN'T EFFECTIVE

SOME PARENTS have difficulty with anger.

For example, if a mother is not confident in her ability to care for her children, she may become emotional and angry when her children cry. She may tell herself, "I shouldn't get angry; I should try to help my child feel better," and she might make an effort to think of her children as adorable, but because she doesn't understand anger, her efforts are in vain. And so the stress builds up within her, and she may become tense and upset. There are even some poor women who become sick from this and even go so far as to try to kill their own children. It is not because they do not have love. But they are beaten from the very start.

Parents who are confident in themselves do not become angry, and no matter how much a child cries or misbehaves, they are able to control the situation. Even when they raise their voice to scold a child, this is just the appearance of anger; they do not become emotionally angry. This is why their words are so effective. They are able to think of the child's pride and ability to reason, and to scold in a way that does not hurt. This type of parent is very successful at raising children.

NOT BECOMING ANGRY WITH A CHILD
IS NOT THE SAME AS SPOILING HIM

TRUE LEADERS never become angry.

Humans in the real sense are devoid of anger. This means that if we are able to learn and master methods for ridding ourselves of anger, we too can become truly human and true leaders.

To be clear: I don't mean that never getting angry means simply accepting everything. I once saw someone's child behaving very badly right in front of her, but the mother thought to herself, "I must not become angry. The monk told me so," and so she just sat and watched as her child misbehaved. Whatever he said or did, she just told him it was all right.

When I saw this, I knew that it was a mistake and could not end well. If you truly love a child, you need to be able to tell him sternly when he is doing something wrong. But this person couldn't even see that a child who behaves in such a way would eventually be disliked even by his own mother, which will never do. This is not the right way to live.

LOVE AND CONFIDENCE ARE WELL REGARDED

WHEN A PERSON has real love and is free from anger, he's able to conduct himself like a king. If he sees someone do something wrong, he can simply say, "That's wrong. You should stop," and that's it. People who do not have anger feel confident in themselves, and so even when they come up against someone who's angry, the encounter doesn't become an emotional conflict. People with reason and compassion are able to see things from the other's perspective and to advise from that vantage in ways that don't injure even an angry person's pride, like sheathing a sword that has been drawn.

Think about times when others didn't listen to you. Weren't those times when you didn't feel love or confidence in yourself? That is why the others didn't listen, no matter how many times you repeated the same thing over and over. But people listen when someone speaks up directly and says, "This is wrong. You should stop," for the speaker is confident and speaks the truth.

We see this happen frequently in the world. The world is confused and confusing because so many people with so little confidence in themselves are speaking and desiring to be heard. No one listens to the words of those beaten by life, and this makes them even angrier. It is no wonder the world is in such a state.

NEVER GET ANGRY,
NO MATTER WHAT HAPPENS

THERE IS A TEACHING known as "the parable of the saw." The story depicts in a vivid way the motto by which the followers of the Buddha live and provides a real method for ridding oneself of anger. But it's not an easy story to accept—only those who are honest can do so.

You may think that nearly everyone is honest, that only a few people are truly dishonest, but the sad fact is that there are very few truly honest people in the world. Many people are working to better themselves, but too often they make no progress. Do you know why? It is because the desire to be a better person is often not an honest one.

People live in the firm and deep-set belief that they are correct. They may tell themselves that they have to try harder, or stop getting angry, or never tell a lie, but these are not their true feelings. What they truly believe is "I am right." What you may think you feel and what you actually feel can be completely different. An honest person is one in whom such contradictions are minimal.

The Buddha said, "If violent thieves captured you, and though you were innocent of anything, took a saw and said 'Let's cut this person in pieces. It'll be fun!'—even though they started sawing you into pieces—you should not become angry in the least. If you do, you're not practicing what I have taught.

So if you wish to be a disciple, you should prepare your mind in this way."

Why did he say this? Because anger is a terrible poison. The Buddha taught that people must be in command of anger even to that extent. It is as if the Buddha were saying, "It is wrong to become angry. Anger is a poison. If you become angry, even at the moment you are killed, it will undo all the merit you might have earned—and you may fall into a woeful state after your death."

You should begin by telling yourself that you will not get angry no matter what happens. If you are able to do that, then you will certainly not be disturbed if someone insults or ignores you, or your in-laws treat you badly, or other such trivial things. If you are able to say to yourself in honesty, "Even if someone were to murder me, I will not be angry at him," then the things that happen in your everyday life will surely not be enough to upset you.

UNDERSTAND TRUE EQUALITY

ALL LIVING THINGS have equal rights. Only their bodies are different, meaning that they live in various ways. If you accept the truth of this equality, you will no longer be susceptible to anger.

Think of it: cockroaches hide in dark places in the kitchen; cats eat the special food their owners buy for them; mice come out at night when everyone is asleep and hunt for scraps of leftover food. But these apparent differences are all no more than the results of the differences in their bodies. Humans walk about their homes without needing to hide or run away, but this too is merely by virtue of the fact that our bodies are built like this, not because we are somehow greater than other things. We are all equal in our status as living things.

This means that we have no right whatsoever to become angry with others. Becoming angry is evidence that one does not truly understand the meaning of equality. All living things have their concerns and their sufferings, and all are of equal value. No one is of special importance. When two different things' needs come into conflict with each other, both will think, "Mine is the right way," and in the end neither will be able to live with the other. But if you become able to see that things are equal—that your worries are yours, but others have their own—your sense of ego will weaken, and your inclination to anger will leave you for good.

Even if the person you are dealing with is your own child,

if you become angry, it is because you do not truly believe that you are equals. The same is true for monks. It would be wrong for us to become angry with initiates. All of our bodies are essentially the same, so no one has the right to become angry with another. The same is true of teachers and students, principals and vice principals—while it may be appropriate to recognize when something is wrong and needs to be corrected, no one has the right to become angry with another.

So if someone above you gets angry with you for no reason, just think to yourself that you'll ignore it. And for people who seem to be below you in society, your attitude should be of working together to solve problems. Being able to employ the concept of equality in this way is a wonderful thing.

DON'T GET HUNG UP ON "REASONS TO LIVE"

MOST OF US have something that we cling to deep inside, something that we see as essential for our happiness. As long as we have that one thing, we feel we can be happy. It may be delicious food, or one's treasured children, or the prospect of being able to travel somewhere nice on vacation. People think of these things as what makes life worth living, or act as if they were the sole reasons to live.

But what happens when these things are gone? Won't your life become very sad? Think of a happy, hard-working mother who says, "I live for my children." Her children will grow and eventually leave home, and when that happens she may experience extreme loneliness, lose her vitality, and become depressed. After that, all that will remain is bitterness. "I did so much for them, giving them whatever they wanted, but now my children pay no attention to me." And then what will happen? She may begin to attack her own son, or his wife, or to lash out at others, until people come to think of her as a nasty old woman. Her body may suffer as well, and soon her life will be full of sorrow. The same is true of people who devote their lives to their companies. They may think that they live for their work, but after their retirement they find they have nothing to do. Loneliness sets in; they grow sick and weak, and then they die.

In order to avoid this, you need to accept all developments and try to enjoy whatever may come your way. Essentially, enjoy work when you have it; when you do not, enjoy retirement. If your grandchildren visit, enjoy playing with them. You need to be somewhat creative to acquire happiness out of ever-changing situations.

There is no need to insist on some specific reason for living. It is just something you decided by yourself, so it is entirely possible to change. Surely you get tired if your grandchildren come, and you play with them all day. When they leave, instead of feeling lonely, you should take a different kind of enjoyment from knowing that you can now relax and take time for yourself. Just think, "Yesterday my grandkids dragged me all over the place. Today I can take it easy," and your fundamental happiness will remain unchanged.

If you can teach your heart not to reject or resist things, whatever may occur, there will be no room in it for anger, and you will be able to enjoy each new day as it comes.

THE EGO IS THE SHACKLE
OF THE SELF

ALL PEOPLE HAVE some kind of position, or title, or ego, but these are no more than shackles.

The ego is like a cross one bears. When the ego becomes a source of pride, it's nothing other than a form of anger—a self-destructive force. For it's certain that not everything will go your way, and becoming angry every time that happens causes harm to the body. People are doomed to suffer for as long as they carry around their egos, which prevent living in harmony with society; indeed, living with ego is the very antithesis of harmonious living.

I am sure you know the story of Jesus Christ's final days, after he had been sentenced to crucifixion. In Jesus's case, he had no choice but to carry on his back the tool used to kill him. But the rest of us happily carry the cross of the ego around with us. We get nailed to it and find no promised land of happiness.

The point of this is to let go of the ego. This doesn't mean you have to go so far as to forget your own name. But if someone asks who you are, you would simply give your name, and nothing else about your position or status. People who introduce themselves as "Jane Smith, the chief so-and-so of such-and-such corporation and director of XYZ," are simply rattling off a list of all the crosses they bear.

LET GO OF SELF-IMPORTANCE

WHY DO YOU think people mistakenly begin to believe in their own greatness? It's because ego has clouded their vision.

If we let go of the ego, we can see clearly and live rightly, and such thoughts will never enter our heads. All you need to do is think to yourself things like "I am nothing special" or "I'm not so important." Even if you have graduated from an Ivy League school, if someone tells you to sweep the floor, just pick up a broom and do it. That is all you need to do.

The reason people get angry is because they have pride and strong egos. Almost all problems would disappear if people could just shed these notions of being president, or boss, or wife, or husband. None of these concepts is worthwhile. If, after getting married, a man decides that he is the one in charge because he is the husband, it will be a lopsided and uncomfortable relationship and cause a great deal of stress in the family.

LET GO OF SELF-LOATHING

JUST AS THINKING oneself to be great is ego, so is thinking oneself to be useless. If you go around thinking that other people have wonderful abilities and you have none, you will be plagued by feelings of envy, and you'll feel angry at those who have what you don't.

But even if you don't have some specific skill or capability, what's the problem? No one said that you have to do any particular job; people who can do it will. It's fine if everyone just does the work they're best suited for.

Once you throw away the notion of "Me, me, me," your problems will disappear. People who aren't good at drawing pictures do not need to draw; let those who are do it. Do people who cannot play piano have a reason to resent, be jealous of, or angry with those who can? Those who can't play should enjoy listening. After all, a talented pianist needs people to listen to her.

If you think of things in this way, anger will disappear. No one in the world is good at everything, so it's fine if every person discovers what he or she is good at, and simply does that.

LET GO OF COMPETITIVENESS

PEOPLE DON'T LIKE to lose.

We often talk about people who can't stand losing. But in fact, such people fall into two categories. The first type can't stand losing to other people, due to their sense of pride or egotism. From the Buddhist perspective such ego is mistaken, and the idea of not wanting to lose to another person is not at all a good thing.

But there is a second kind of person who can't stand to lose but doesn't have any feeling of ego. These are the people who can't stand losing to themselves. They may get upset at not grappling with a problem seriously enough, or be disappointed in their own failings, or be ashamed at not having done what they should have. But as you can see, this arises not from the ego but from a sense of self-discipline. We have to work diligently to sustain our lives.

DOING YOUR BEST IS ENOUGH

EVERY DAY we face challenges such as jobs that need to be finished or meals that need to be cooked. We shouldn't do such things in the hopes that someone will congratulate us for doing them. We should do them with the sense that something worth doing is worth doing well.

When cooking, for instance, our goal should be to make a meal that will be enjoyed by all, a meal no one could complain about. You might say that this feeling is one of not wanting to lose, but the competition is with oneself, not other people, and that is fine.

Remember, it is enough if people simply do their best at the jobs they have to do. There is no need to think about winning and losing against others. But please do not lose against yourself.

DON'T LET SETBACKS MAKE YOU ANGRY

WE GET ENJOYMENT from life when we succeed at things we have done. So thinking of ways to complete your tasks and do them well is a lovely way to live. If you make your plans and fulfill them, one by one, your record of little successes will mount up, and you will feel good. By stringing together the many small units of achievement you have planned and accomplished over the years, you can make a wonderful life for yourself.

Anger will interfere with plans, and the moment you become angry, your plans will begin to fall apart. Anger can arise very quickly. When writing a letter, you may make a mistake or spell something wrong and for the slightest moment feel angry that things are not going well. Or when using a machine, you may want to kick or punch it if it doesn't work as you want.

Getting angry is the same thing as losing—which is no fun, because it's an experience of unhappiness. But if a person does not become angry even when there seems to be ample reason to do so, that person can be considered a true winner. In your own life, you should commit yourself every day to not becoming angry from the very instant that anger begins to arise. If you can do this, the things that were frustrating you will go your way. When you do this, remember that you are prevailing over the situation. You will go from losing to winning.

FOCUS ON UNDERSTANDING, NOT ANGER

ANGRY PEOPLE lose in life. There is nothing wise about them. They are simply heaps of anger moving about. But if you can see anger the instant it appears and observe it calmly, wonderful things will begin to happen. You will be able to look at whatever problem is at hand and reason out how to deal with it, including how to prevail over other people's anger.

Imagine that two people are arguing over whether something is A or B. It would be a mistake for a third person to come along and say, "She is right. He is wrong." Instead, you should say, "Let's look at this to see if we can't answer the question together," and so find a way to work through it and quell any anger that might have arisen. I often use this approach myself. When listening to other people's problems, one needs to consider many things, but even so, it's usually possible to quickly resolve even the thorniest difficulties.

The point is not to get caught up in the other person's anger but instead focus on the actual problem. Don't get distracted into thinking how bad some person is for becoming so enraged and using strong language. Instead, think to yourself, "This person is showing such and such an emotion, while that person is showing some other emotion. But the real problem is X." Then tell them both, "This is the problem. What do you think of such-and-such solution?" After you have let go of your position, wants, and opinions, people will become very receptive to your suggestions.

DEFEAT ANGER WITH WISDOM

FROM TIME TO TIME people who love to argue with or complain about each other come to me and begin telling me that something between them is wrong or causing them problems. I don't allow them to speak emotionally, but ask each to tell me what the problem is and how it is troubling them. After that, most people say very little. And once they begin reflecting on the actual nature of the problem, their minds settle, and they can start to comprehend more clearly. Once they're calm, I say, "If that's the problem, perhaps you could try this?" And they generally agree. After resolving the issue, I ask them if they have anything else they want to say, but for the most part they no longer do and leave together as friends.

This is a case of wisdom triumphing in a situation that otherwise might have taken hours of heated argument to resolve. It feels good for me to be able to achieve this, and it helps to reduce the number of angry people in the world. In short, this is letting wisdom prevail over anger. Seeing how wisdom can do this is interesting, and it makes one more confident in oneself to be able to use it in this way.

Anger means losing. And it is very easy to win against a person who is quick to anger.

BECOME LIKE A CRYSTAL BALL

In order to make yourself impervious to anger, you need to be able to do one more thing: know how to respond when someone does something that absolutely deserves to cause anger.

Now, if some person were to do bad things in his or her own little world, then there would be no need for anger; we could just watch and smile and explain what that person was doing wrong. The problem arises when others do bad things that affect you. People may hurt, abuse, mock, or discriminate against you even when you have done nothing wrong. What should you do in such situations?

Most people think it would be foolish simply to sit there and smile. But remember that no matter what someone does to you, by allowing it to make you angry you are validating his behavior. If people call you a fool, or worthless, or irresponsible, and you become angry, you are acknowledging what they say. Even if they make up some slander about you, the slur does not say anything about the real you. You should simply listen and let people say what they want.

Think of yourself as a ball made of smooth crystal. If you're a crystal filled with light from within, no matter what mud or filth someone may throw at you, you'll wash off easily. If you can keep that image in your heart, you'll be able to shrug off any attack with equanimity. But if you soak everything up like a sponge, you are doomed to lose.

STERN LESSONS ARE NOT THE SAME
AS ANGER

OF COURSE, if someone does attack you, you should firmly point out his or her error.

A sternly worded lesson is not the same thing as anger. There are a few people in society who seek to cause problems for others, but such people are simply ignorant. Telling them to stop whatever wrong thing they're doing and letting them know that you will take action if they do not is entirely appropriate.

Although you should not become angry, this does not mean you have to shrink away from problems. Rather, you should have a bigness of heart that is entirely free from anger. So even when you speak sternly, you must do so without anger, or the anger will defeat you. If you speak in anger, the words will have no effect, for you will have descended to the same level of ignorance as the other person.

SHOW THE SELFISHLY WILLFUL
A MIRROR

PLEASE REMEMBER that it's better to remain calm and without anger. When someone behaves violently, abusively, or selfishly, simply show him or her a mirror. Do not become angry yourself. Showing an angry person his or her face in the heat of anger should be a very frightening experience.

And how does one get another person to look in the mirror? Suppose a person is angry and yelling at you. If you try to defend yourself or yell back, you have swallowed that same poisonous anger. This means you have done exactly what the other person sought to make you do, and you've been beaten by anger.

The better approach is just to hold up a mirror and say, "I can see that you are very angry. That must be very uncomfortable. Your hands are shaking. It seems that you get angry easily. That certainly must make things difficult for you. Are you all right? I'm worried for you." Simply make your explanation in a spirit of compassion and without passing judgment. The person you are dealing with will not expect this; the strategy of anger will have failed, and the person who had been angry can begin to calm down. This approach can result in happiness for both sides. This is what is meant by "showing a mirror."

LAUGH, AND ANGER DISAPPEARS

Wɪsᴅᴏᴍ ɪs necessary to cure anger, and laughter is a companion of wisdom.

You can't truly laugh and be angry at the same time, so try to laugh as often as you can. The first thing to do is tell yourself you want to live a life full of laughter, then promise to laugh out loud, without embarrassment, whenever something strikes you as interesting or funny, and then follow through with it. It looks easy to do but is more difficult than you might think.

Laughter and anger are polar opposites. Once you have vowed to laugh at everything, even when you begin to feel anger, all you need to do is remind yourself to laugh. This will help you to rid yourself of a great deal of anger. Just don't forget to keep smiling, and make laughter a part of your life.

It's often said that laughter helps in the recovery from illness. Patients who laugh feel better inside, have a more positive outlook, and even their immune systems are better at fighting off disease.

THE WISER YOU ARE, THE MORE YOU LAUGH

I'VE MENTIONED many times that anger is the depth of ignorance; similarly, laughter is the sign of wisdom in action.

Why do we laugh? Obviously because something strikes us as funny. Sometimes something is humorously funny, but there are also times when things are funny in an incongruous way. Therefore, laughter can be a sign that you have recognized something that is unusual or peculiar, meaning you have avoided ignorance or dullness of wit. But anger is the opposite, a display of deep ignorance. In order to laugh instead of becoming angry, you need to be able to replace ignorance with wisdom and knowing.

Many cultural forms, such as theatrical plays, songs, and stand-up routines, have been developed to make people smile and laugh. Think about examples of these objectively for a moment, and resist the urge to laugh while thinking about what it is about them that people find amusing. You will see that the person who created the comic work has studied and understood human behavior and found a way to turn it into something we can laugh at.

WISDOM AND UNDERSTANDING LEAD TO LAUGHTER AND HAPPINESS

BEING ABLE to make people laugh is not a sign of silliness at all. It takes insight and a real gift to make people laugh—it's a tough job. It means understanding that people usually act a certain way in some situation, and then being able to turn that on its head. Finding the opposite of a conventional, commonsense approach is a good way to make others laugh, and this means that when they do laugh, they are using their heads and really looking at the way things are.

But there are those who just don't seem to laugh at anything—they simply don't get it. Some people have no sense of humor. And how do we think of them? We usually say that they don't understand anything; they can't even get a joke. They cannot share in the understanding that makes things funny.

In any case, laugh as often as you can. You will be happy the moment you begin, and it will make you healthier, more beautiful, and better loved by others. Cosmetics and dressing fashionably cost lots of money, but laughing doesn't cost a cent to make you happier, more beautiful, and richer in the most important way.

WISE LAUGHTER, FOOLISH LAUGHTER

You do have to be careful in laughing. When I say, "Laugh to be happy," it does not mean the same thing as "Laugh because you are happy." The two are completely different.

Laughing just because you're happy can be a dangerous thing. This is a sign of your own ignorance and can lead to disaster. People who laugh thinking, "I'm so lucky. I've got whatever I could want: money, everything," often come to misfortune. The reason is simple: the world does not work that way. It's impossible to have complete contentment when you live a life defined by your desires. When people like this start to become satisfied, it only makes them want more, which eventually leads to their downfall. People who think everything in their life is perfect— no problems at work, no problems at home—are simply fortunate fools. Their laughter stems from ignorance.

Please try to avoid confusing wise laughter with pitifully ignorant laughter. Happiness does not come from simply laughing like a fool. Use your wisdom to think about and laugh at the world as it really is.

DON'T MAKE LAUGHTER YOUR GOAL

ALTHOUGH YOU SHOULD certainly laugh, don't make laughing your mission in life. Laughter isn't a goal to be achieved or something that you do all the time to the detriment of work and other important things—laughter isn't an opiate, which distracts with pleasure.

Right laughter is not laughing just because you feel that you want to laugh, nor is it laughing just because you are happy. It's genuine laugher. Some people want to laugh so much that they go out to see movies or comedy shows just so they can laugh. They can't laugh at home by themselves, so they have to go out and look for it, even pay for it. Isn't that strange? You should laugh at home or outside, when things go well or when they don't. True laughter can be carried with you wherever you go. You shouldn't need to leave home to find it.

LEARN TO LAUGH, AND THE WORLD IS A FUNNIER PLACE

HOW CAN YOU learn to really laugh? The easiest way is just to start laughing, right now. At first it may not be so easy to laugh whenever you think about it, but if you work at it, you can learn to make yourself laugh.

The funny thing is this: even if you're just forcing yourself to laugh, after a while, you'll begin to notice lots of other funny or interesting things. Your power of insight will begin to strengthen. People who are happy all the time are people who see interesting things wherever they look.

Look at children. They'll find something to play with if you leave them to themselves for a minute. They don't care where they are or where you take them; they just need something, anything will do. But only the very young seem to have this gift. It's easy to make babies laugh. All you need to do is say, "Peek-a-boo!" I doubt they even know why they're laughing. Maybe they just think, "Mom looks happy, so I guess I'm happy too."

FUNNY THINGS ARE EVERYWHERE

ONCE YOU COMMIT yourself to laughter, it's not difficult to find funny or entertaining things to laugh at. There are strange and fascinating aspects to everything. Nothing in the world is perfect, which means there's something funny about everything.

But in order to convince people of this, I usually have to show them myself; if I just talk about it in words, they don't understand. So I say to them, "All right, now I'm going to laugh all by myself," and just start laughing. I don't show the reason; I just think of things that make me laugh.

You really can find something interesting about anything. If you just remember that nothing in this world is perfect, you'll always be able to find something to make you smile. For instance, when it's raining and I board a train and roll up my wet umbrella, I'll sit and watch as the drops of water trickle down and drip to the floor and try to guess which direction they will shimmy off to. One goes one way, and then, when the train brakes, another veers off in a different direction. It's actually quite fun watching the beads and trails of water set off on their little adventures across the floor of the train. You learn a lot from it. And if the water isn't moving anywhere, you can use the tip of your umbrella to poke it into different shapes. People sitting around me may not notice what I am doing, but I do this kind of thing often.

Laughter is the signature of power, and anger the seal of defeat. If you want to be happy, start laughing now. You'll leave anger behind, and anger is the thief of happiness. The wise always choose laughter. There's nothing difficult about it.

USE UNDERSTANDING RATHER THAN ANGER

UNDERSTANDING IS KEY. This does not just mean understanding things by using the knowledge you have in your head—it also means grasping situations and what led up to them.

First, you need to keep calm. For example, if a child starts to say she doesn't want to go to school, most people just say, "Well stop fussing about it. You have to go anyway." But this response is in fact from a feeling of anger. If you don't let the situation disturb you and instead try to understand it, you will begin to reflect that there must be a reason your child does not want to go to school.

People who cannot make this leap are mired in senseless and selfish worries about how their children need to be able to study, or how the neighbors might start gossiping, or how the other children living nearby don't complain in the same way. Parents may simply demand that the child goes to school, but try to remember that children are individuals, not just the slaves of their parents.

If this were to happen, the first thing you should do is just say, "Oh, really?" and then take a moment to give yourself a chance to think about the situation. When you realize that there must be some reason for your child not wanting to go, your heart will settle and you can begin to think more clearly. This will remove the concern from your face and allow you to listen with a smile, and your child will sense that immediately. Then ask if there's a reason why she can't go to school, or if there is something you can do. If she says no, ask if she wants to talk about it. When she is talking, take care not to fall back into thinking only of your own position. If you remain on her wavelength and try to work it out together, a solution will appear.

Sometimes your spouse might come home in a bad mood and may even say something mean to you. But if you react by getting angry yourself, the situation will just get worse. Instead, just recognize that he or she is in a bad mood today, and your mind will become calmer and you'll be able to ask about why that is.

The same is true at the office. Perhaps some person is trying to improve his sales and goes it alone, instead of sharing information with anyone else. Some bosses might get flustered, worrying about the effect this will have on morale, and, without thinking about the reasons, order the employee to start filing reports and working with the team. But someone with a clearer head would wonder whether the person was doing it out of a true sense of hard work, or simply out of pride, or because he didn't want people to discover that he was actually incompetent. Once the cause is understood, the solution becomes clear. If the problem is actually negligible, it may be fine just to let it continue. If it seems to be threatening the company, you might assign the person to another job.

This kind of understanding is actually another way to free yourself from anger. In the same way, if you make a mistake but someone scolds you more severely than you deserve, don't just get upset or make a sour face, but think to yourself objectively that you made a mistake and now the person seems to be overreacting.

DEALING WITH ANGRY PEOPLE

You may be making progress in your practice of not becoming angry no matter what happens. But you'll find that even though you don't become angry, others around you will. What should you do in such situations?

The answer is to make yourself even calmer than usual and look at things with objectivity. If your boss at work becomes angry with you, try the following approach. Think to yourself, "This person is speaking to me as my boss. I made a mistake at work, and now he has to talk to me in this way for it. If I were in his position, I'd probably have to do the same thing. He is the victim, not me." The same is true for relatives who can't get along. If a wife has friction with her mother-in-law, for instance, the wife should think, "She's the victim here. She used to be in charge of everything as the mother, but now someone else has come in and taken her son and that authority away from her. Now she is alone." Once you're able to see and understand things in this way, the solution to the problem will become clear.

You could also try thinking of yourself and the other person equally as victims. If someone is bullying, abusing, or ignoring you, recognize that it's out of a sense of his own inability or lack of confidence, and he wants to belittle you to compensate. If you look at the situation clearly, you'll feel sorrow for such a person, not anger.

DON'T INGEST SOMEONE ELSE'S ANGER

ANGER CAN SNOWBALL—angry people tend to get angrier and angrier. People who cannot stop becoming angry must find a way to spit out the poison as it builds up within them. They do this through angry speech. Such speech can cause problems for those around them, but there is nothing wrong in simply listening.

Think of an incompetent boss who is always being cruel to a competent younger employee. If the employee just listens and thinks to herself, "This man is getting old and can't do his job well. I worry him, so to get rid of his stress he keeps doing these things. I should help him get out of that pattern of behavior," she is responding in just the right way.

Listening doesn't mean getting swept up in an angry person's emotion. The other person is just spitting up garbage they've ingested; there's no need to swallow it yourself. Becoming angry is just like having a stomachache from eating something bad, and angry words and actions are just regurgitation. The angry person needs to continue until he or she is free from the poison, but there is no reason for you to eat what that person throws up. No one wants to eat something that has been vomited by someone else—this is how you should think of other people's anger. Angry people first get angry themselves, then try to cause anger in others, as if they are trying to make other people eat their vomit.

The answer is simply not to eat it. Remember this when you feel yourself being drawn in by another person's anger. You need to avoid it as you would avoid something disgusting. If you can keep this in mind, you will be able to free yourself from being contaminated by other people's anger.

LOSE ANGER, FIND MIRACLES

IF YOU'RE ABLE to avoid becoming angry at others who are angry with or abusive to you, you may find them transformed into allies and friends—so that everyone wins instead of fighting. In attacking you, remember, people only hurt themselves, so just keep smiling and understand that people are free to feel as they wish; their emotions are out of your control. Even when people are furious, if you're able to keep smiling, you may find that somehow their anger will gradually soften and they may even smile as well. You can become friends, and they may never get angry with you in that way again. This is a powerful energy that can seem miraculous. You may even find its effects difficult to believe.

Additionally, once you're free from the taint of anger, you'll find yourself growing in confidence as well. You'll begin to feel freedom from the poisons of desire and ignorance and get a taste of the fruits of knowledge and wisdom. And prevailing over these poisons will leave you feeling happier and stronger. These poisons cause nothing but grief and suffering for yourself and others, so by defeating them, you bring peace and calm to yourself and those around you.

PEACE IS THE LANGUAGE OF THE STRONG

WITHOUT TRUE COURAGE, angry people attack others with violent words. Societies that spend their time trying to build ever-more-powerful weapons show the same cowardice and self-doubt. The converse is also true; when we free ourselves from anger, we become strong.

Those who advocate peace are strong; those who compete and can't stand to lose are weak. Courage is needed for peace.

ANYONE CAN BE HAPPY

ANGER IS UNHAPPINESS. I want all people to be able to live happily.

There's no need to worry or be upset for a minute or even thirty seconds. Fill your heart always with joy, and you'll feel bright and clear and enjoy life. Life is too short for suffering and sorrow; enjoy it! All it takes is the right attitude—anyone can be happy.

We just need to keep that source of unhappiness known as anger from entering our hearts. The instant we learn to do that, we get a real taste of joy. And by practicing ways to keep anger away, we grow in wisdom and learn to see things as they are. Learning how to not get angry by following your wisdom is a pathway to happiness in life.

ABOUT THE AUTHOR

 **VEN. ALUBOMULLE SUMANASARA,** a Buddhist monk schooled in the Theravada tradition, has written more than one hundred books addressing the practical application of Buddhist thought and practice to daily life.

Born in Sri Lanka in 1945, he became a novice monk at the age of thirteen and was ordained in 1958. After teaching Buddhist philosophy at the University of Kelaniya, he went to Japan in 1980 to study Japanese Buddhism on a fellowship from the Sri Lankan government, pursuing his doctoral studies at the graduate school of Komazawa University. In 1994 he established the Japan Theravada Buddhist Association, through which he continues to spread the Dharma and lead others in the practice of vipassanā meditation.

Sumanasara's sincerity and gentle manner, as well as his facility as a speaker in both English and Japanese, have earned him a broad following. Focusing on the fundamental teachings of Buddha, he explains how Buddhism offers down-to-earth wisdom that anyone can put into practice to better understand and manage the challenges of the here and now.

ABOUT WISDOM PUBLICATIONS

WISDOM PUBLICATIONS is the leading publisher of classic and contemporary Buddhist books and practical works on mindfulness. Publishing books from all major Buddhist traditions, Wisdom is a nonprofit charitable organization dedicated to cultivating Buddhist voices the world over, advancing critical scholarship, and preserving and sharing Buddhist literary culture.

To learn more about us or to explore our other books, please visit our website at www.wisdompubs.org. You can subscribe to our eNewsletter, request a print catalog, and find out how you can help support Wisdom's mission either online or by writing to:

Wisdom Publications
199 Elm Street
Somerville, Massachusetts 02144 USA

You can also contact us at 617-776-7416 or info@wisdompubs.org.

Wisdom is a 501(c)(3) organization, and donations in support of our mission are tax deductible.

Wisdom Publications is affiliated with the Foundation for the Preservation of the Mahayana Tradition (FPMT).

ALSO AVAILABLE FROM WISDOM PUBLICATIONS

DON'T WORRY, BE GRUMPY
Inspiring Stories for Making the Most of Each Moment
Ajahn Brahm

From the bestselling author of *Who Ordered this Truckload of Dung?*

A HEART FULL OF PEACE
Joseph Goldstein
Foreword by the Dalai Lama

"In this short but substantive volume, Joseph Goldstein, who lectures and leads retreats around the world, presents his thoughts on the practice of compassion, love, kindness, restraint, a skillful mind, and a peaceful heart as an antidote to the materialism of our age." —*Spirituality and Practice*

WHEN THE CHOCOLATE RUNS OUT
Lama Thubten Yeshe

"Lively and enlightening."—*Spirituality and Practice*

SAYING YES TO LIFE
(Even the Hard Parts)
Ezra Bayda with Josh Bartok
Foreword by Thomas Moore

"Astonishing."—*Spirituality and Health*

INSPIRING GENEROSITY
Barbara Bonner

"I am amazed every day by the stories of people around the world who give of themselves to help others. *Inspiring Generosity* is a beautiful book."—President Bill Clinton

NOW!
The Art of Being Truly Present
Jean Smith

"Every saying in this book is a good tool for meditation."
—*Eastern Horizon*

FIRST INVITE LOVE IN
Forty Time-Tested Tools for Creating a More Compassionate Life
Tana Pesso with His Holiness Penor Rinpoche
Foreword by the Dalai Lama

"*First Invite Love In* is a clear, practical handbook that will genuinely help anyone who reads it and follows its exercises."
—Sharon Salzberg, author of *Lovingkindness*